brilliant

personal
effectiveness

Douglas Miller

Harlow, England • London • New York • Boston • San Francisco • Toronto • Sydney • Auckland • Singapore • Hong Kong
Tokyo • Seoul • Taipei • New Delhi • Cape Town • São Paulo • Mexico City • Madrid • Amsterdam • Munich • Paris • Milan

PEARSON EDUCATION LIMITED

Edinburgh Gate
Harlow CM20 2JE
United Kingdom
Tel: +44 (0)1279 623623
Web: www.pearson.com/uk

First published 2015 (print and electronic)

© Douglas Miller 2015 (print and electronic)

The right of Douglas Miller to be identified as author of this work has been asserted by him in accordance with the Copyright, Designs and Patents Act 1988.

Pearson Education is not responsible for the content of third-party internet sites.

ISBN: 978-1-292-07756-7 (print)
       978-1-292-07758-1 (PDF)
       978-1-292-07759-8 (ePub)
       978-1-292-07757-4 (eText)

British Library Cataloguing-in-Publication Data
A catalogue record for the print edition is available from the British Library

Library of Congress Cataloging-in-Publication Data
Miller, Douglas, 1966-
   Brilliant personal effectiveness / Douglas Miller.
      pages cm
   Includes bibliographical references and index.
   ISBN 978-1-292-07756-7
   1. Communication in management. 2. Communication in organizations. 3. Interpersonal communication. 4. Interpersonal relations. I. Title. II. Title: Personal effectiveness.
   HD30.3.M54 2015
   650.1--dc23
                                    2014039843

10 9 8 7 6 5 4 3 2 1
18 17 16 15 14

Illustrations by Bill Piggins
Series cover design: David Carroll & Co.
Print edition typeset in 10/14pt by 3
Print edition printed and bound in Great Britain by Henry Ling Ltd, at the Dorset Press, Dorchester, Dorset

NOTE THAT ANY PAGE CROSS REFERENCES REFER TO THE PRINT EDITION

Contents

About the author

Douglas Miller is a writer, speaker and trainer who currently works in more than 20 countries on four continents. *Brilliant Personal Effectiveness* is his ninth book. He can be contacted at: doug@douglasmillerlearning.com

A full profile can be found at:
www.douglasmillerlearning.com

Author acknowledgements

I would like to thank the following: Rebecca, Christian, Mo, Kristina, Robin, Mike and Paddy who allowed to me to use quotes in relation to personal effectiveness which I have featured in the introduction to this book. A warm thank you to lecturers at the University of East London, particularly Christian van Nieuwerburgh and Julia Yates, for inspiration. And to Elspeth Campbell (**www.elspethcampbell.com**) for alerting me to Barnett Pearce's work.

I would also like to thank the following at Pearson Education; Steve Temblett who commissioned the book and offered sage advice on content and Laura Blake who took the book from manuscript to market. The remaining errors are mine.

Publisher's acknowledgements

We are grateful to the following for permission to reproduce copyright material:

Figures

Figure on page 66 adapted with the permission of Simon & Schuster Publishing Group, a division of Simon & Schuster, Inc. from the Free Press edition of BE EXCELLENT AT ANYTHING: The Four Keys to Transforming the way we work and live by Tony Schwartz with Jean Gomes and Catherine McCarthy, PhD. Copyright © 2010 by Tony Schwartz. All rights reserved.

Text

Text on pages 39-41 ©Copyright 2004-2014, VIA Institute on Character. Used with permission. All rights reserved. www. viacharacter.org; Brilliant Example on pages 53-4 from *Make Your Own Good Fortune*, BBC Active (Miller, D. 2006).

In some instances we have been unable to trace the owners of copyright material, and we would appreciate any information that would enable us to do so.

Introduction: What is personal effectiveness?

'If thy heart fails thee, climb not at all.'

Elizabeth I, monarch

When I started this book I thought it would be a good idea to circulate a short questionnaire about personal effectiveness. It is such a wide subject that I hoped that asking people what it meant to them would provide focus. The replies were very interesting but also, in a sense, frustrating because it became clear that it meant different things to different people. So, before you read on, a question to ask yourself now is quite simply: 'What does personal effectiveness mean to me?' You might also want to think about the things you currently do to maximise your own effectiveness. Planning your day properly when you get in to work might be one example, how you work in a team another, but the ways you maximise your own effectiveness may be different from these examples. From my perspective, if I ask myself the question 'What is personal effectiveness?' I immediately start thinking about 'interpersonal effectiveness' – things like how I communicate, how I assert myself and how I try to influence others. These are all covered in this book.

It became clear that there are some things on some people's radar that probably do not exist on others' radar at all. Perhaps the interpersonal element, valued by me, does not even register with you. Perhaps you see your effectiveness in terms of how you plan, prioritise and organise yourself. You might work in a marketing or sales department and your effectiveness in part is dependent on how you sell yourself – making a great impression or delivering a presentation. Perhaps so much of what you do is on a computer screen that your virtual online presence is critical. Of course there is no wrong answer here and every answer is therefore right.

So any one definition of 'personal effectiveness' will not resonate with everyone and, if we could capture it in sentence or two it might be so bland as to be meaningless. It means different things to different people. So, instead, I think it is best left to those who sent me their definitions of what it means to them. Here is a selection of the comments that were made.

> One group of responses related to overcoming psychological blocks. Two comments illustrate this:
>
> ● 'Dealing with negative emotions and learning to control them', and
>
> ● 'Confidence has always been an issue for me. When faced with a new task or project my initial thoughts are "I won't be able to do that".'

To that end, the opening chapter deals specifically with over-coming these psychological blocks through unlearning what we call 'false scripts' in our minds which may be hindering progress. However, one of the intentions of this book is to build confidence in the areas of working life where you need to be at your most effective so the chapter is also very clear about how you can best learn to do this.

Chapter 2 looks at two elements without which personal effectiveness will be a real struggle. The first is the true engagement needed with whatever you do; without this you cannot hope to be effective. One of the key factors here is that we truly engage with those things that have the deepest meaning for us. These are what coach and learning expert Tim Gallwey calls 'the source of our potential... the seed from which our lives grow'. With this in mind the second part of this chapter is about what those 'seeds' might be for you. There is a 'walk-through' of Martin Seligman and Christopher Peterson's work on 'character strengths and virtues'. There is also an online questionnaire developed by them to support this where you can get a profile of your own character strengths (**www.viacharacter.org**).

An interesting comment came from one respondent who said it would be great if there was some sort of formula which could help you assess how effective/impactful you might be in a given situation. Well, now there is. The formula says that your effectiveness comes from the excellence of your strategy combined with your likelihood of success. This also features in Chapter 2.

A second group of responses looked at the issue of what's known as 'time management' but which I prefer to call 'managing yourself' (you can't manage time, it's finite). Here are two examples of comments:

- 'Getting stuff done, overcoming procrastination' and
- 'The tasks you enjoy and are good at you do quickly and effectively so they take up less time, but the things which need to be done but you don't enjoy or find hard you procrastinate about, take longer over them than you should and they are a drain on your time and energy as a result.'

Chapter 3 covers the core principles of managing yourself in terms of how you use your time and includes a look at that primary time thief – the misuse and abuse of email. It was interesting too that issues around health incorporating mental and physical well-being were important and 'well-being' is also a feature of the chapter. The comment above included this ('a drain on your... energy') and the commentator below stressed the values of positive 'energy' and directing it in the right way:

> 'Personal effectiveness makes me think of "efficiency". I believe we all have a finite amount of "energy", and for me, personal effectiveness is associated with the positive use of energy in a way that has an "impact". I find that some activities that I undertake use up energy, but generate enthusiasm and positive feelings which help to re-fill my energy levels. Some other activities use up energy, but do not generate enthusiasm or positive feelings. In those circumstances, the energy is "wasted".'

Chapter 4 covers goal achievement and the setting of timelines that help us to achieve our goals. One comment, 'how to get rid of emotions that hinder me from achieving my goal' was a typical one. The chapter does however also emphasise that some aspects of life should be open to experimentation. If innovation and creativity are seen as a key part of organisational futures then for you to be effective in this future will need more open, fresh thinking. Thinking in this way is featured in this 'Goal achievement' chapter (with the emphasis on developing opportunity-taking and problem-solving goals) but also in Chapter 7, 'Working in a team'.

The next batch of comments concern our relationships with those we work with and in particular, in this case, how we are seen by them:

> 'I've noticed how some people seem to have more credibility than me. People listen to them, take them seriously.'

This respondent together with several others refer to different aspects of communication skill and this issue is covered in Chapter 5 'Communication essentials'. Credibility underpins effectiveness in areas like assertiveness and influences and this comment illustrates the challenges some of us have:

> 'I find myself being very hesitant with certain kinds of people. Saying "yes" when I know I should be saying "no". I still do this even though I am in my forties, really struggling to say what's on my mind.'

Chapter 6 'Assertiveness and influencing' covers assertiveness itself and connected subjects such as influencing where the previously mentioned 'credibility' is so important. A key focus is to look at typical situations we find ourselves in at work and how we can be effective in those situations. To this end the chapter looks at the all-important 'mental rehearsal' you go through prior to challenging situations such as dealing with a 'difficult' person and preparing to speak at a meeting where you want to exert influence.

And finally, this comment from someone who raises an issue that one survey said more people are afraid of than death itself:

> 'Whole careers seem to be have been made from being able to speak well in public. So, I'd say speaking and presenting with real impact is so important.'

Rather than devote a chapter to this specifically I have chosen to apply the topic of speaking in public – be it at a team meeting to a few colleagues through to a speech to 500 people – as a working example across several of the chapters in the book.

How the book is structured

There is a clear structure to this book. The first four chapters are concerned primarily with 'you' and your own personal effectiveness. Although nothing happens in isolation there are a number of things, such as planning and organisation, where the focus is on the self. This forms Part 1 of the book entitled 'Improving your personal effectiveness'.

The second part, entitled 'Improving your impact on others' concerns the way you improve your impact on others. Communication and team skills are a part of this, with a whole chapter, Chapter 7, devoted to team-working.

There is a third, shorter part to this book ('How to make a virtual impact') which is solidly 21st century. Our virtual world is, some would say, as important as our physically inhabited one. Remote or virtual teams are now commonplace and we need to communicate just as we did before but in situations where we are not in physical contact with other team members. We also need to have an online presence through social networking tools such as LinkedIn. How many of us utilise this tool and others like it, for maximum professional benefit? Internal communication and networking tools such as Yammer need to be used in the right way, for the best effect. Even the humble email, that much-used and much-abused communication tool is now so central to our working lives that it is almost impossible to remember how we ever managed without it, though no doubt those who receive hundreds of emails a day wish we still did. All these issues are covered in the final part of this book in Chapter 8 'Working in a virtual world'.

'The reward of our work is not what we get, but what we become.'

Paulo Coelho, novelist

PART 1

Improving your personal effectiveness

CHAPTER 1

Learning and unlearning

'If everything was perfect you would never learn and you would never grow.'

Beyoncé Knowles, singer

To borrow and distort a George Orwell quote, every chapter in this book is equally important but some are more equal than others. There is little that is more important in our quest for impact than the power of learning. It's the very reason you picked up this book and the reason it has been written. For example, every interaction you have with other people has the capacity to change you in some way and, by extension, change the other person too. If you have a productive conversation with someone you previously found 'difficult' you may discover that your behaviour may have been at least partly responsible for this or the other person has a completely different view of the world which you had not even considered before. And that view is just as valid as your view. You've learned something. Your effectiveness over time with others will come from learning to adapt your behaviour to different people. You learn and you've changed.

'The person has all these false and distorted social masks and myths – 'I'm a rotten person, I'm no good, I can never do anything right' – all these false scripts that are self-defeating and injurious.'

Ken Wilber, writer and developmental psychologist

Learning is a skill in itself and if 'learning to learn' sounds a bit weird consider also that we sometimes have to 'learn to unlearn' (bad habits, unhelpful mind-sets) as well which might sound even weirder. The quote from Ken Wilber warns of a danger in that to learn effectively many of us have to change the self-narrative from a defeatist one, which says we hold untruths about ourselves in our minds, often based on one or two bad experiences in the past, and which we carry around with us potentially for life. The mind-set goes: 'The way I am now is the way I always will be.' This needs to be unlearned before true learning and insight can occur. Happily, while many of us display some of the characteristics of the non-learner in certain aspects of our lives, in others we are completely the opposite. We are great learners. But we can also be great non-learners.

In this chapter we are going to look at two aspects of learning. The first is how we can overcome the 'set mind': 'I am as I am.' The second is the things we can do on the way to being top performers. This section will use examples from across all aspects of high performance including sport and musicianship and includes the crucial element of how you receive feedback.

Receiving feedback can be a huge catalyst for new learning or it can result in defensiveness, denial and a consequent drain in confidence. In fact, to return to an earlier theme, some feedback received early in one's life, given with the best of intentions (though possibly given badly), can be carried through as a piece of self-narrative, the 'false script', for the rest of our lives. At this point, before we look at learning mind-sets, you may want to think about some of the assumptions that you have about yourself that are based on single experiences or an isolated piece of feedback. These might include anything from the presentation you gave which didn't go so well to lack of self-confidence generated by the excellence of others ('I can't do that' ergo 'I'm hopeless'), to an event in your school years such as being embarrassed in class when you didn't know something. You have the choice to either make this false assumption come true (the perfect self-fulfilling fallacy) or to challenge it by saying 'I don't have to be like that' and opening your mind to what you can do to negate the false script.

brilliant tip

One of the things that is noticeable in high performance is the way in which certain people use the achievements of others as inspiration while others generate diminishing statements about the inferiority of themselves as though their lack of success in certain areas will go on forever and is therefore a fait accompli. The question to ask is 'How can I use the excellence of others as a catalyst for my own improvement?' Questions like, 'What does the good presenter do that I can learn from?' or 'She's so good with people. What is she doing that I don't do well at the moment?' As a regular swimmer I can attest to the inspirational effect of two-time Olympic champion Rebecca Adlington on my own efforts. I noticed her breathing technique when she swam the freestyle and it made all the difference to my own stroke (and speed).

Set mind or new mind-set?

'Skills and abilities alone do not predict performance, but what you believe you can do with what you have, under a variety of circumstances, has the greatest impact.'

Albert Bandura, psychologist

You are what you are, not what you intend to be

So right away let's have some contradiction. The introduction to this chapter made clear that some of us are not really as we think we are. We've made ourselves as we are through a bad experience, sensitivity to criticism, the comparative success of others and (although the jury's out on this one) a disposition to lack of confidence. So, in this sense we are what we are. It's what the outside world sees. So, this person, even though they have the capacity to be so much more than they are now, doesn't know or believe this and therefore fatalistic thoughts and feelings are reflected in under-performance.

Recognising this is only one step. Challenging the set mind and then adopting new mind-sets about what you can be triggers the process by which you then become the person you intend to be. The person you intend to be is the real, authentic you, not the previous one you assumed you were. If we do nothing, then we only ever stay as we are. And that is all we will be. So, easily said, but what are the barriers to this? How do we overcome the blocking beliefs that create false 'me'?

Prove yourself wrong

It's a laudable human trait that we prove ourselves right. If you believe something to be true you begin to selectively sift the evidence to prove the self-opinion. So, a self-narrative that goes 'I am hopeless at managing myself' prompts us to look at all the times when we were thoroughly disorganised and didn't get the important stuff done. What we tend not to do is to look at the evidence that challenges the self-view. There will be times when we did plan and organise with beneficial consequences and this can be used as a counter-argument to the 'I am hopeless' statements.

Usually it's not lack of capability at all but simply lack of knowledge that hinders. Here's a classic example. Lack of confidence in public speaking can come from bad experiences but even in speeches with little impact there are usually some things done well. This author has seen speeches delivered that failed because of the poor way in which visual aids were used (we've all been subjected to 'presentation karaoke' where the speech is mostly embedded in the slides and the speaker reads the slide for us, as though we are unable to do so ourselves). It's not that the speaker is unable to speak/present to a group. It's simply that the speaker has no idea of the impact that his or her poor use of visuals is having. A little knowledge and learning makes all the difference.

This works equally well as an insurance policy against over-confidence. Even in things that have gone well, disprove your own brilliance. There is always scope for improvement. Only the arrogant fail to recognise vulnerability.

Change your language

Proving ourselves right is one human trait. Using exaggerated language to explain ourselves to ourselves is another. We've already used an example of this with the self-critical words 'I'm hopeless'. Psychotherapists talk of the way in which we catastrophise bad experiences. The poorly received presentation was not 'a disaster'. It was a setback, but if you resolve to learn from the setback it is extremely unlikely to occur again. As tennis player Boris Becker once said when losing at Wimbledon in the early rounds, 'nobody died', and of course he then gave himself the chance to understand why he lost and to practise so he could do better at next year's tournament.

If you have a bad experience, cool, rational analysis of what happened serves you so much better than the sweeping statement that allows no scope for learning and improvement.

With so much of our professional effectiveness and impact coming via others this generalising language doesn't serve us well in our relationships either. It's not helpful to refer to others in general terms.

Change your conversation

Just as some generalise internally about themselves others generalise externally. If you say something about yourself enough times people start to believe it about you. They then reinforce the view back to you which further cements that self-view in your own mind. If you say 'I can't do this' others believe it and you don't get the chances you need to get better. 'Pat doesn't really like saying very much at team meetings' (a consequence of Pat saying this to a colleague) means that Pat doesn't get invited to speak which means that Pat never gets the chance to learn, improve and build her confidence.

brilliant example

Tim Gallwey is a pioneer coach and an expert in learning and performance. He wrote a seminal book many years ago called *The Inner Game of Tennis*, which created a huge shift in the way we think about how people learn best to increase performance levels. In more recent years he has written *The Inner Game of Work*. The idea of the inner game is that we have 'two selves'. Self 1 is the 'teller' – the person in you who gives you the orders, i.e. 'do this' or 'do that' including self-criticism and self-praise. If you have decided to commit to learning to do something better you will always be talking to yourself in the context of this desired improvement. Self 2 is the 'doer' – the person who acts on those instructions. Self 1 is always talking to self 2 in the bid for improvement.

However, Gallwey says that self 1 often contaminates self 2 by this endless 'do this, do that' instruction which inhibits self 2 from learning naturally. We have within us a 'silent intelligence' that, in Gallwey's words:

'is an inner intelligence which is staggering. What it doesn't already know the inner intelligence learns with staggering ease. It uses billions of memory cells and neurological communication circuits.'

Self 1 mistrusts self 2 which is why it issues so many instructions. Because of the number of these instructions self 2 risks becoming paralysed by so many messages. Ever heard the phrase 'paralysis of analysis'? Self 1 stops the naturally intelligent self, who has the answers, from putting them into practice.

What we get from this is that our best performance at work, leisure and indeed when playing tennis (the source of Gallwey's original ideas) comes from your potential (far greater than you may think) minus the interference (self 1). The interference, often negative in a person who lacks confidence or who has had a bad experience, is a serious barrier to improvement.

Gallwey, being a tennis coach, originally noticed how, by letting tennis players practise their game naturally without 101 instructions from as him as a coach, they would revert to their silent intelligence as a means of improvement. The performance improvements were dramatic.

This doesn't preclude advice, recommendation and suggestion – after all what would be the point of this or any other book like it if that were the case – but you must give your natural, silent intelligence the chance to work without overloading it with messages. Practise with purpose, listen to advice and experiment, but appreciate that we learn best when we allow for what psychologist and educationalist Guy Claxton has referred to as 'the slow way of knowing'.

By the way, it's also self 1 that is responsible for all those negative statements we send to ourselves referred to earlier: 'I can't do this', 'I will never be able to do this', 'I'm hopeless'. This is the potentially contaminating self 1 doing its worst.

Succeed at failing

Failing is great. In fact it's so good that Richard Fenton the author (with Andrea Waltz) of *Go for No!* suggests that we should actively try to increase our failure rate. The logic to this argument is that if failure is almost always the prerequisite for success then surely it follows that you must increase your failure rate to increase your success rate.

Although there are a few salespeople out there who can sell anything to anyone, what most good salespeople know is that the first step in successful selling comes purely from the number of people contacted. The principle in contact-centre selling is that you contact ten people, get rejected by seven leaving three who want to know more and one who eventually buys. Contact a hundred people in a day and you get ten sales (but please don't call me...). That's ninety failures in a day. Contact twenty people and you get two sales. That's only eighteen failures. But only two sales.

Michael Jordan, perhaps the greatest basketball player of all, says in his book *Driven from Within*:

'I've missed more than 9000 shots in my career. I've lost almost 300 games. Twenty-six times I've been trusted to take the game-winning shot and missed. I've failed over and over and over again in my life. And that is why I succeed.'

The point about failure is what we do with it. Do we use failure as a catalyst to succeed next time or do we accept failure as an end point – confirmation of what we expected of ourselves? Do we say instead that failure sits in the middle of a continuum with you at the beginning and success at the end? It's not for nothing that the classic statement 'without failure, success is not an option' has become more popular. It's about saying that failing does not make you a failure and succeeding at something, anything, makes you a success.

You are going to fail at work on a regular basis. So now that we have established that failure is a good thing – you may well have been convinced of this anyway but perhaps not in such stark terms – what are the things we can do to turn failure into success?

1 *Failure tests your desire to succeed at something.* To succeed
at anything – making that great presentation, having
an impact at meetings, influencing colleagues more
effectively – requires true engagement with the thing you
want to succeed at. That usually means lots of hard work
and hard work tests desire. You only work hard at the
things you truly want to get better at. Later (in Chapter
2) a model is presented to help with this process of true
engagement.

*'What on earth would make someone a non-learner? Everyone is
born with an intense drive to learn. Infants stretch their skills daily.
Not just ordinary skills, but the most difficult tasks of a lifetime,
like learning to walk and talk. They never decide it's too hard or
not worth the effort. Babies don't worry about making mistakes or
humiliating themselves. They walk, they fall, they get better.'*

Carol Dweck, author of *Mindset*

2 *Failure tests what's known as your 'explanatory' style.* When
something doesn't go as planned we attempt to explain it
to ourselves and attribute the failure to one of two groups
of factors. The first will be internal factors such as beliefs
about oneself, personality issues and general disposition.
The second covers external factors such as unknowable
'events', genuine bad luck, peer pressure and societal
norms. Fritz Heider, one of the first great thinkers on
this, says that we place too much emphasis on the internal
factors. So, as we have already seen, the person who fails
and sees him- or herself as a consequent failure is doing so
as a result of attributing that setback to something innate/
fixed within him- or herself that cannot be changed, e.g. 'I
am no good at walking into a room and engaging strangers
in a conversation.' If this is a fixed view then there is little
scope for saying, 'If I try X, Y and Z I give myself a very
good chance of getting better at this.'

Internal factors however, are important, but they need to be positive and proactive rather than an expression of a fixed level of capability. It's good to say, 'The reason I failed is that I didn't give myself a chance to do this properly because I didn't practise enough' and then to say 'so a solution here is that I need to practise more next time.'

Setbacks sometimes do have very good external reasons for their occurrence and genuine bad luck can be the cause (e.g. bad weather). One former British prime minister said that 'events' were always the thing he feared the most because it's so hard to plan for them. In some environments the external pressures are so strong – societal pressure to conform, for example, or working in an organisation that has a particularly dominant personality which makes it hard to initiate new projects – we already have the odds loaded very heavily against us. An extra layer of preparatory thinking is needed to increase the odds of success.

In attributing these external factors to setback and failure, do listen to the tone of your 'head chatter'. If your story seems to be an ongoing one of bad luck perhaps it's providing a convenient excuse when actually the reasons for the setbacks lie within you.

brilliant tip

People can fail at success. Saying 'I got lucky' or 'anyone can do this' does not attribute any of the reasons for success to internal factors such as practice, hard work or insightful thinking. Ask 'What did I do to make a difference?'

3   *Don't be afraid to make mistakes.* Mark Brown, whose book *The Dinosaur Strain* is one of the very best books on

personal and professional success (and referred to several times in this book), talks of two kinds of mistake: the 'sensible' mistake and the 'stupid' mistake. The stupid mistake might be one where we do the same thing over and over again in the hope of it eventually having a different outcome (incidentally this was Einstein's view of insanity). This ties in with our desire stated near the beginning of this chapter to prove ourselves right, or one where we don't make the right adjustments to give a better chance of success next time if the first approach hasn't worked. A stupid mistake might also constitute breaches of safety, legality or ethics/morality (such as offensiveness to others at work).

A sensible mistake is when we did something honestly trying to do something good. As someone once said, 'anyone who isn't making any mistakes isn't trying anything'. What's important is that we learn from those mistakes and don't just repeat them. An alternative is that we make adjustments to what was inherently a good idea to give it a greater chance of success next time. For example, you try something new in a team meeting such as meeting standing up (lots of organisations do this) but see that people get tired after ten minutes. So the next time you add some high tables that people can lean against (much like we do in bars).

▶ brilliant example

There is a big point to all of this. You are reading a book on improving effectiveness and impact at work because it presents a learning opportunity for you. As reading a book is a relatively passive learning exercise it needs to turn into an active one for it to have its own impact. Along with the suggestions in this book you will have many of your own ideas about

▶

maximising your own impact and will want to put them into practice. As you do this the thinking behind success and failure will apply to you in your quest to be more effective. Not everything will work first time, or even at all. You will 'shape' and 'mould' your progress as though you are working on a piece of pottery on a potter's wheel. Some ideas won't come off, some will. And even when it's finished on the wheel the pot goes on changing as it is decorated with glazes and fired in a kiln.

If you can learn from failure, keep improving and making adjustments when you need to then you maximise your own chances of success - in this case your personal effectiveness and impact at work.

Your true capability

Testing out your true level of capability is tough but what we do know is that so many of us underestimate this and as a consequence miss out on opportunities. An interesting example of how this plays out is demonstrated when you ask people to think about what they are capable of – perhaps you can consider this question now for a few moments.

Many immediately interpret that question as an invitation to look back over their life so far, writing down a list of previous accomplishments and enjoying the feeling that life has had some successes. Just a few people will also see the bigger potential in the invitation and will think also of capabilities yet to be revealed or developed further or things that excited them when they were younger which got 'lost' in their teenage years and which they want to return to. Many people however, see the invitation as a personal history lesson – at its extreme some are already saying to themselves, 'I am only capable of doing the things I have done.'

As people get older, they look back at previous achievements and define their capabilities. As your personal history gets longer your future gets shorter. This is a massive barrier to future learning if capability is seen in terms of the past and not in terms of future potential as well. There is no reason, when being asked this question a second time ('What are you capable of?') for a few things on that list not to have a future focus.

We looked at the danger of false scripts in the opening to this chapter. A more accurate script should say:

I am fully able to learn and develop my capabilities for the rest of my life.

These capabilities are potentially unlimited.

Kickboxing

Gary Hamel is one of the world's great thinkers on organisational strategy and success. He is of the view that innovation is one of the critical 'what matters now' factors in organisations (it's hard to find anyone who disagrees with this) and by extension people who can think in new and refreshing ways are going to be highly valuable to employers in the future to kick-start this innovation. For some at least, this means learning to think in new and refreshing ways.

The phrase 'thinking outside the box' has become so common that it's in danger of becoming a cliché where the original meaning becomes lost in its thoughtless repetition. So, to bend this a little, but also keep to its original, very good, idea I advocate 'kickboxing'. The box stands for habits, ideas, products, services, that represent the routine, conventional and 'normal' and from time to time this box needs a good 'kicking' – in thought at least. But how do we kick it best? And how do we unlearn the desire to make the box last forever? Try the Brilliant exercise below. This exercise can help us learn new patterns of creative thinking and also to understand simultaneously why we often get locked in the thinking of the past.

 exercise

This exercise takes about three minutes and you need three sheets of paper and a pen. You will need to draw three things, one on each sheet of paper. It is not a test of your drawing ability in any way so do not shy away from the drawing element because of your perception of your drawing ability. Ignore the false script that says 'I can't draw.' Although it is tempting to just read on if you can please do try to perform the exercise – it makes the learning from it that much stronger.

It goes like this:

1 You own a shoe manufacturing business and you are about to exhibit your new shoe design at the Milan Shoe Fair. Please draw the shoe that you will be exhibiting. Take a minute or so to draw it and please don't read on until you have.

2 Put the drawing to one side for the moment. OK, you've sold that business and decided to set up a new business...

3 Your new business manufactures CD boxes. Can you draw your design for your latest CD box? Take a minute or so to draw it and please don't read on until you have.

4 Put the drawing to one side for a moment. OK, you've sold that business too and decided to set up a new business...

5 This is the final drawing. You have set up a new business that sells mobile phone shakers. Please draw a picture of your new mobile phone shaker that will go to market. You should not fear being wrong. Draw what you like. And please, once again avoid the temptation to read on until you have finished.

OK, so what are you thinking? Probably 'What on Earth is a mobile phone shaker?' And then maybe you either thought the author was stupid for asking you to draw something that doesn't exist or you yourself were stupid for not knowing what a mobile phone shaker is. As far as this author is aware a mobile phone shaker doesn't exist so in effect, as the artist, you are being asked to invent something. So, how did you do? Did you give up because you didn't know what it was or did you have a go anyway?

Let's look back at the first two drawings and then come back to the final one. With the first drawing you were asked to draw something with which you were familiar, which already exists, and therefore, if you look at the drawing now it is obviously some kind of shoe/boot. With the second drawing there is a little more ambiguity. Is it a box for holding one CD? A box for holding lots of CDs? Possibly a piece of furniture which looks good in your lounge and holds lots of CDs? If ten people are asked to draw this simultaneously there will be a variety of different designs, but the fact is that we all know what a CD is and we are being asked to design some form of container which we also have a mental frame of reference for.

So now back to the mobile phone shaker. If you drew this you probably tried to make a connection between the word 'phone' and 'shaker' and went from there. Once you felt comfortable with your new challenge you did it, but some won't. This chapter is called 'Learning and unlearning' and this last part of the exercise requires you to 'unlearn' some things.

- **The past**. Being a prisoner of the past prevents us from entertaining the possibilities of the future.

- **That 'wrong' exists**. Take away the fear of being wrong (or of making a mistake – see above) and it is amazing what we can create. There is no such thing as 'wrong' for example in creative thinking.

- **Feeling silly**. As you were on your own doing this the fear of looking silly might not have been there, but put ten other people in the room performing the same challenge and you may have felt differently.

- **The false script**. So we return to the theme at the beginning of this chapter to finish this section. The false script in our heads with this exercise goes along the lines of 'I can't do that' or 'I can't draw so I won't do it' or 'I don't know what it is so I won't have a go' or even 'the author is a fool', but, in truth we can all say (and this author is sure that some of you did say):

'I can do'

'I can try to draw'

'What does it matter if I don't know what it is, I can have a go anyway?'

'If I'm not wrong what I have I got to lose and if I am wrong it's only a picture anyway?'

brilliant recap

- You are what you think you are.
- You are far more capable than you think you are (even if you think you are capable of a lot).
- Change the conversation you have with yourself about yourself. Avoid 'false scripts'.
- Failure is a necessary prerequisite for success.
- Things happen over which you have no control. Work on the things you *can* control.
- Capabilities are not just based on past provable experiences but also on 'future capabilities to be developed'.
- We create a fulfilling future if we aren't afraid of letting go of some of the past.
- Have a go – there's nothing to be lost and much to be gained.

Performance excellence

'The way I see it, if you want the rainbow, you gotta put up with some rain.'

Dolly Parton, singer and entrepreneur

It was once claimed that real expertise comes from having made every mistake it is possible to make. As we have seen in the last section, mistakes are an essential part of the learning and unlearning process on the road to becoming a skilled performer.

There seems to be a small number of good habits that most experts agree on and the aim of this section is to condense those and give them meaning in the context of work. This section will reference a number of very enjoyable, thought-provoking books and several academic studies and, if you wish to read further and more deeply into how to improve your own performance standards they all come highly recommended.

First, however, we reference a pioneering work on excellence in performance which many writers on securing top performance cite. It was truly ground-breaking. Psychologist Anders Ericsson and two colleagues at the elite Berlin Music Academy asked the professors at the Academy to divide the Academy's violinists into three groups. The first group comprised the truly outstanding who could become world-class soloists. The second group were very good musicians in their own right who could perform in top orchestras but were unlikely to be renowned soloists. The final group featured violinists who weren't quite good enough to perform in top orchestras and were likely to become music teachers. The relative levels of proficiency were assessed as objectively as possible.

After a rigorous series of interviews a fascinating pattern emerged. Between the ages of five and eight (most started playing at the age of five) there were no significant differences between the groups in the amount of practice they did. From the age of eight there were still strong similarities (number of teachers for example) but one huge difference then began to emerge. By the age of 20 those in the first group had averaged 10,000 hours of practice each, those in the second group around 2,000 hours less and those in the third group a further 4,000 hours less.

As the icing on the cake, there wasn't the natural who 'bucked the system' – that is rose to the top with far less practice than the peer group. All of those in this top group had consistently clocked up around 10,000 hours of practice.

Here comes a key point which just doesn't get said enough and we all must consider in our endeavour to perform better. To perform at a high standard – as a leader/manager, a musician, a salesperson or an athletic sprinter – you have to work hard and the heights you reach will depend on the amount of work you put in. To perform at the very highest standard you have to be truly dedicated to excellence.

So, hard work is a prerequisite for high performance. What else is required? In continuing this section we look at the additional characteristics required for you to be a top performer:

- practice with purpose
- tapping into excellence
- feedback.

A number of other areas have already been covered in the context of high performance earlier in this chapter and one in particular is the removal of the 'false script' – the self-conversation that says 'I am as I am', 'I cannot improve' and worse still 'I am hopeless'.

Practice with purpose

Deep practice is built on a paradox: struggling in certain targeted ways – operating at the edge of your ability where you make mistakes – makes you smarter.

Daniel Coyle, author of *The Talent Code*

There are lots of talented people who don't get anywhere. As we've seen with several examples in this chapter, if you want to be good at anything, you have to work hard at it. Indeed, more research is revealing substantial evidence for the overarching importance of hard work when set against talent. Practice with purpose demands three things of us.

1　The desire to get better – whether it's managing people, giving excellent presentations or working on advanced computer programs in an ICT department – must be sincerely and deeply held. This desire is always tested – sometimes very, very hard indeed. If you didn't make it, it's nearly always because you didn't want to 'make it' enough to put the required hours in as part of the learning process. The desire will come in part from authentically connecting with what it is you are doing. The best ICT people are the ones who love what they do – historically think of Apple, Microsoft and Google (and incidentally, Bill Gates and Steve Jobs spent thousands of hours in their garages at homes mucking around with early computers and code because they loved it). The best people managers are the ones who work at their empathy skills and are willing to receive feedback from those they manage (see 'Feedback' below). While there are some presenters who seem to be able to speak without thinking, for many there exists the paradox of 'prepared spontaneity'. Speakers work very hard at making the words right (and the body language and tone of voice). You've got to love your subject, love speaking or want to do it enough (or all three) to put in the hours of practice needed to be good on your feet.

2 Practice with purpose means taking the time to focus on particular aspects of your performance. If you are aiming to develop your public speaking skills, rather than trying to work on five things simultaneously try to concentrate on one specific aspect of the overall skill such as voice projection or body language (the sort of things that can be done in front of a mirror). As we shall see later (in Chapter 3 on managing yourself, the section on well-being in particular) experts in performance improvement talk now of intently engaging to improve and then completely disengaging to restore energy levels. As Geoff Colvin, the author of *Talent is Overrated* says:

'Deliberate practice requires that one identify certain sharply defined elements of performance that need to be improved, and then work intently on them.'

3 Performance improvement means pain before the pleasure of success, effectiveness and impact. Failure, setback and the sheer investment of time is, as we have already seen, part of the recipe of high-level performance. But seeing yourself in the future, doing the thing you are working on (what we call 'self-actualisation') can be used by you to drive yourself through the 'pain' – actual or metaphorical. By the way, if that 'future you' doesn't interest or, better still, inspire you – stop now. Go and do something that does. It's a short life and you're wasting it.

Tapping into excellence

In his book *Bounce* author and journalist (but formerly a world-class table tennis player) Matthew Syed talks about his formative experiences.

brilliant example

Matthew Syed was Britain's number one table tennis player for a number of years. He initially thought, as he says, that he became good through a combination of 'speed, guile, gutsiness, mental strength, adaptability, agility and reflexes' and those things were innate. His success of course had to be based partly on those things but where did they come from? Was he born with those attributes or did they develop, over time, in another way? It's the kind of story many top performers tell themselves and although there is some truth in the idea that certain innate attributes play a part in the story of success it seems that another critical factor is at play.

However, on closer examination things looked a little different. Syed goes on to talk about his childhood. The street he lived on all through his formative years, Silverdale Road in Reading in the UK and its local vicinity went on to produce more than ten national champions at different levels over the course of very few years. They all knew each other and practised together. Was it by chance that that single locality in Reading produced, at a point in the 1980s, more champions than the rest of Britain combined? Syed accounts for the success of Silverdale Road in the following terms:

'if a big enough group of youngsters had been given a table at eight, had a brilliant older brother to practise with, had been trained by one of the top coaches in the country, had joined the only 24-hour club in the county, and had practised for thousands of hours by their early teens, I would not have been number one in England.'

This supports much of what the research into performance excellence (including Anders Ericsson's violinists) tells us about hard work and practice but there are several other factors we can pinpoint which will serve us well in the bid to perform at the highest standard.

- Syed had an elder brother to perform with who was initially better than him. He had many other peers who were excellent performers and they developed and grew alongside each other. Where you can attach yourself to top performers you will see your own standards rise above the level they would have, had you been among lesser performers. As we change jobs more frequently than we used to, think also about working for 'excellent' organisations. The best organisations have the best people. The best organisations are also able to provide the resources to help you rather like Syed always having a table available for him.

- Syed had a great coach who just also happened to be a teacher at his local school so he and his mates had a top-class coach to call on. If you want to improve at anything source the people who can really make a difference to you. There has been a huge boom in executive and business coaching over the past ten years. Contemporary coaches believe we are our own best problem-solvers and the best coaches aim to work with us to bring out the internal facility we have to overcome challenges. You have the answers in you – a good coach holds up a mirror to you and helps you bring out the best in yourself. Mentors have a role too (mentors will have answers – not necessarily *the* answers) and you can ask a successful, more senior person who has credibility in your eyes to mentor you.

● Syed refers to the '24-hour club'. They practised whenever they could.

You may attribute much of Syed's success to luck – having a peer group to develop with, a coach, facilities and time – and in his case there is an element of truth to it. But for top performance, we make our own luck and many of the points we've made here around hard work, desire, willingness to learn and surrounding yourself with excellence are things you can control. Put yourself in an exceptional place – make your own luck. There aren't enough great people to go around but you can be one of them if you want to be. As Geoff Colvin says:

'for virtually every company, the scare resource today is human ability.'

 **recap**

   ● To be a top performer you need to work very hard.

   ● Excellence in you does not have an end point - talent might provide a slightly advantageous start point but does not predict the end point.

   ● To be a top performer you have to *want* to work very hard. If you don't want to work to get better you won't.

- Many top performers, although they describe the process of learning as being, in some ways, 'painful' also in hindsight talk of the enjoyment of the journey.

- 'Future you' is a great motivator as long as the future 'you' is the authentic 'you'.

Feedback

We've looked at blocking mind-sets in this chapter – particularly in relation to the false scripts we relay to ourselves. This also occurs in the receiving of feedback. In research for a previous book, *The Luck Habit*, I was fortunate enough to interview a number of top performers in the realms of business, sport and music. One thing that united them more than any other was their willingness to receive feedback and the way they subsequently used it. This is a critical factor in your professional development and for the top performers it was, in almost all cases, the giving of feedback that provided a seminal moment in their own performance improvement.

You've probably already had plenty of feedback and you're going to get lots more but it will rarely be given in the way you want it. It might be personal ('you let people walk all over you'), poorly timed (ages after the 'event' or in the middle of a mini-crisis), vague ('You're not good on the detail are you?') and even without the opportunity to reply – as though the feedback was beyond debate and further discussion. Let's be clear however, there are people who give feedback very well and this may be more akin to your professional experience.

So, what's your role? What can you do to make the receiving of feedback a vital cog in your desire to improve?

Use it positively

Feedback – whether criticism or praise – should always be a positive experience. That doesn't mean it always is. It may be given badly and leave you with a loss of confidence, baffled or even resentful. Badly given feedback is not your fault but the way you respond to any feedback is your responsibility. Feedback is often given vaguely or refers to personality issues. This is unhelpful so the onus on you is to make it useful to you. This is not a criticism of the giver. It's just that most people don't know how to give feedback in a way that is most beneficial to the receiver.

Prove yourself wrong

Just because feedback can be badly given – non-specific, personality rather than behaviour-based – it does not invalidate it. Rather than expecting perfection in the giver help the giver to do it better. Ask for specific examples: 'OK you've said I am very passive in meetings. Can you give me one or two examples when this was the case?'

brilliant tip

If it sounds as though feedback is all about what could have been done better it's also about what has been done well. Although I think most of us would agree that praise isn't given nearly enough – if you are a manager or have management aspirations do take note – when it's given to you, thank the giver. Those who lack confidence are prone to receiving praise badly. 'Yes, but that was really easy', 'You're just saying that, Sam was much better than me' or 'No, didn't I do this bit badly?' are common retorts. If this is you really try to acknowledge what has been said positively.

You choose how you use

Feedback is opinion. The opinion may be entirely right but it's up to you to decide what you do with it. The course of action you take should be 'considered' and you shouldn't be rushed into making commitments that you subsequently regret – just saying 'I need time to think about this, I wasn't aware of it' if it's criticism is perfectly legitimate. It sends a signal that you've listened (even if you don't agree). In the heat of the moment, particularly when we receive surprising information, the reaction is emotional and few of us think at our best when emotions are heightened. You can disagree with what has been said (in your own mind) but don't dismiss what has been said without further thought. It may be something you were aware of anyway, perhaps someone has said something similar before or you might just think 'Do they have a point?'

 **recap**

- You 'happen' to a feedback conversation – don't be a passive receiver of feedback.

- Feedback is often (but certainly not always) given badly. Make it better by asking for specific performance-related examples.

- Relate feedback to a specific experience and ask yourself how you would do it differently/better next time.

- Ask for feedback. How do you know how you're doing without it?

- Feedback, whether praise or criticism, is valuable for learning and performance improvement. Always thank the giver.

- Take time to consider how best to use feedback.

CHAPTER 2

Engagement and effectiveness

'About the only thing that comes to us without effort is old age.'

Gloria Pitzer, 'The Recipe Detective'

I n work, as in life, your effectiveness comes from the mental (and sometimes physical) resources you are willing to apply to whatever situation you are in. This willingness will depend on how engaged you are in what it is you are doing. If what you do doesn't engage you then there is little chance that you will do what needs to be done to be effective and make a difference. So what do we mean by engagement?

brilliant definition

Engagement occurs where the effort we make, the involvement we feel and the effectiveness (or 'efficacy') of our actions combine so that we meet our personal objectives and, in the context of work, meet the objectives of our employer. In a work context, your employer's objectives and the access to things that mean most to you, within you, should overlap.

Finding the SPARC

Extensive research has found that the effort and the involvement needed for engagement comes from five core sources.

1 **S**elf-determination – I exercise control over what I am doing.

2 **P**urpose – I can see the point in doing what I am doing.

3 **A**lignment – I am doing what I want to be doing.

4 **R**eward – I get 'something' from what I am doing.

5 **C**hallenge – I learn and grow while I do what I am doing.

As you can see, the letters in the sequence form the word SPARC. You can think about these five needs even within the context of reading this book. Your engagement with the book will come from the following.

1 Self-determination – I read the book when and where I want.

2 Purpose – I have reasons for reading it.

3 Alignment – reading the book connects with the things that are currently important to me personally and/or professionally.

4 Reward – I can see how I can apply the advice to my own working life for my benefit.

5 Challenge – I am learning as I go along, sometimes I am stretched.

Of course, if you find yourself disengaging from this book – and I hope you don't! – it is likely that at least one of the five SPARC needs you have is not being met.

So, in a perfect world, if you can take care of these five 'needs' you are likely to feel more deeply engaged in what you do and as a consequence your impact and effectiveness will increase. A reasonable response might be to say that we don't live in a perfect world so how realistic is it to hold these five needs up as the ideal? Is the ideal unobtainable?

The purpose of this first section is to look at these five needs in more detail and to explain how you can make them a realistic proposition in your working life. You can extend these five needs into your personal life as well – your approach to hobbies and interests is a great touchstone for providing inspiration for your professional life too.

↗) brilliant impact

The SPARC is an ideal but the creation of the SPARC in your own working life is not a passive activity. It's tempting to be fatalistic and say that just because I have little control and choice over how I do the work I do, i.e. lack of self-determination, that I am therefore disempowered and therefore justifiably disengaged. Looking for perfection is unrealistic. At least part of the onus therefore falls back on us as individuals to, for example, set our own goals (thus creating 'purpose'), to take responsibility for own learning (presenting our own 'challenges') and look for rewards in creative ways such as valuing the good feeling we get from helping someone else as part of a team, for example (see Chapter 7) or enjoying the innate feeling of pride that we get from a job well done.

As we have seen, SPARC is an acronym for true engagement in whatever it is you want to do. In this section we look at each of the five needs in turn and how you can apply them. Some of the themes presented by each of these needs are developed elsewhere. For example 'Purpose' is often expressed through the setting of goals, timelines and deadlines and Chapter 4 covers this. 'Challenge' through learning featured earlier (in Chapter 1).

S – Self-determination

Writer and thinker Dan Pink suggests that we engage best when we have control over the four 'T's.

Task (what I do)

Time (when I do it)

Team (who I do it with)

Technique (how I do it).

We all want some autonomy, some freedom to exercise control and true self-determination comes from autonomy and control. But here's the important bit for you and me – we aren't all the same. We vary in how much control we need. You will need to self-audit here and assess how much you need in principle. Are you someone who likes to work in your own 'zone', to be left to 'get on with it', or are you someone closer to the other end of the spectrum, someone who likes to be directed by someone else?

So, if an element within self-determination is about exercising control what happens in the many situations when you don't have so much control? You might be asking yourself this question already – perhaps your manager is dominant or you work in a very controlling organisational culture. The answer is just as we exercise control we also exercise choice. Self-determination can also mean that we agree to lose a degree of control because we see the advantages of, for example, in working in a team, where there will be compromise, and that our best interests will be served by this. So, here you have the option to change yourself in response to your circumstances.

'the job at which one works is not what counts, but rather the manner in which one does the work. It does not lie with the occupation but always with us, whether those elements of the

personal and specific which constitute the uniqueness of our existence are expressed in the work and thus make life meaningful.'

Viktor Frankl, psychotherapist and author of *Man's Search for Meaning*

If you have to compromise on the level of preferred self-determination beyond the point you can bear you will not be happy in the job, you become less effective (or worse still ineffective or perhaps destructive) and in those circumstances you must move to an environment that suits you better.

P – Purpose

There should be a point to what you do. It could meet a higher goal or it's a simple stepping stone. The purpose might be that what you do is useful to someone else, a colleague for example, or something that contributes to the effectiveness of the organisation you work for. Later (in Chapter 4) we take many of the issues around 'purpose' and present methods for developing goals, for milestones and for goals related to solving problems and taking opportunities.

A – Alignment

I am often asked 'How can I motivate myself?' When I probe deeper I find that the question is driven by current demotivation or dissatisfaction with whatever it is the questioner is doing now (rather than an abstract, philosophical question) and that usually means the job currently being done. There are things that are done at work that help you be a little more motivated and therefore a little more engaged – better pay and benefits, a decent working environment are examples, but these really only get you to some kind of base level.

What really makes you engaged at the deepest level is that what you do connects with the essence of 'you' – your deepest inner treasure, your values and the things that really mean the most to you. This is known as 'alignment'. It's remarkable and saddening that many get to their ends of their lives with little real sense of what these things are for them personally. Before you think more deeply about your innermost treasure there is an important point to be made.

We all have different personalities – seven billion beguiling and endlessly interesting personalities in one world. We are engaged in different ways and by different things. We have things that make us want to express ourselves right away and things that leave us feeling inert and inactive. To be at your most effective in the medium and long term you need to match your work with your passions. We can deal with a disconnection in the short term but beyond that it becomes tough. Earlier (in Chapter 1) we looked at the two 'selves' identified by coach and learning expert Tim Gallwey. Confidence comes from not allowing self 1 (the teller) to sit in judgement over self 2 (the doer). Gallwey introduces a third 'self'. He describes this third as 'the source of our potential... the seed from which our lives grow'. Alignment is quite simply providing a match as far as is possible, between what you do and your third self.

We need to feel that what we do is special to us regardless of how far we might be motivated by the collective pursuit of a goal. We are not talking about perfection here. The alignment doesn't have to be perfect – some people make compromises and do things they don't like doing because they can see the benefit to their career. Others will find the need to compromise – if it goes on for any period of time – too tedious or even painful (the unwillingness to inflict 'soul damage' on ourselves).

So, what about you? What constitutes your own personal treasure? What are the seeds from which your own working life will grow?

World-leading positive psychologist Martin Seligman and his colleague Christopher Peterson have invested time and research in looking at what they call 'character strengths and virtues'. These are listed below. There are 24 of them and they are positive strengths. Using an online questionnaire (**www. viacharacter.org**) you can get a clear sense now of what your own character strengths and virtues are. At the end of the questionnaire you will get a descending scale from those strengths which most closely equate to your own 'personal treasure' down to those least associated with the deepest 'you'. The top five on this list comprise your signature strengths – the real autograph of your deepest strengths and virtues – and it's the accessing of some of these (a minimum of three seems right) that creates alignment and therefore engagement in what you do. The 24 strengths are grouped into six areas and listed below.

1. Wisdom and knowledge

Cognitive strengths that entail the acquisition and use of knowledge.

- Creativity – originality, ingenuity.
- Curiosity – interest, novelty-seeking, openness to experience.
- Judgement – critical thinking.
- Love of learning.
- Perspective – wisdom.

2. Courage

Emotional strengths that involve the exercise of will to accomplish goals in the face of opposition, external or internal.

- Bravery – valour.
- Perseverance – persistence, industriousness.

- Honesty – authenticity, integrity.
- Zest – vitality, enthusiasm, vigour, energy.

3. Humanity

Interpersonal strengths that involve tending to and befriending others.

- Love.
- Kindness – generosity, nurturing, care, compassion, altruistic love, 'niceness'.
- Social intelligence – emotional intelligence, personal intelligence.

4. Justice

Civic strengths that underlie healthy community life.

- Teamwork – citizenship, social responsibility, loyalty.
- Fairness – treating all people the same according to notions of fairness and justice; not letting personal feelings bias decisions about others; giving everyone a fair chance.
- Leadership – encouraging a group of which one is a member to get things done and at the same time maintain good relations within the group; organising group activities and seeing that they happen.

5. Temperance

Strengths that protect against excess.

- Forgiveness – forgiving those who have done wrong; accepting the shortcomings of others; giving people a second chance; not being vengeful.
- Humility – not regarding oneself as more special than one is.
- Prudence – being careful about one's choices.
- Self-regulation – self-control.

6. Transcendence

Strengths that forge connections to the larger universe and provide meaning.

- Appreciation of beauty and excellence – awe, wonder, feeling lifted by what's around you.
- Gratitude – Being aware of and thankful for the good things that happen.
- Hope – optimism, future-mindedness, future orientation.
- Humour – playfulness.
- Spirituality – faith, higher purpose.

Source: **www.viacharacter.org**

R – Reward

Alignment gives your work personal meaning. If you love what you do because it connects with deepest 'you' then your work becomes personally meaningful for you and brings great and lasting reward. But reward comes in many more immediate forms as well. For you it could include:

- the feeling of pride at a job well done
- your innate competitive instincts satisfied
- proper remuneration for the job you do
- helping someone to do their job better
- learning opportunities
- praise from your manager and/or those further up the hierarchy
- thanks from work colleagues – 'I was noticed!'

Feel free to add to this list. There's an old saying: 'If money is the only thing we come to work for then it's the only thing we get.' Engagement demands that the rewards are far greater than this if it's to be sustainable. You will spend up to 100,000 hours of your life in some sort of work. The personal rewards over that period of time need to be substantial for you.

C – Challenge

While the routine is necessary in some parts of your life, true engagement occurs when you are able to stretch yourself beyond what is normal and comfortable. Not so much that achievement feels unobtainable or unrealistic but not so little that you can't start even the smallest motivational 'fire'. For you, this 'challenge' is presented by new learning opportunities. (If you have 'jumped' to this chapter you will find it useful to refer back to the previous chapter which covered both 'learning' and 'unlearning'.)

Being there and being alive

As we have seen there is a world of difference between being present at work and being deeply connected/truly engaged in that work. We have looked at the factors, through the SPARC acronym, that the best research tells us go from being present at work to being truly alive at work. So, how do you know that you really are engaged? Academic Nancy Rothbard (Rothbard, 2001) talks of the difference between being attentive to your work (good) and being absorbed by it (great). Absorption means true engagement. In the two lists below ask yourself into which you are more likely to fit.

Attention	Absorption
I spend a lot of time thinking about my work	I lose track of time
I focus a great deal of attention on my work	I am completely lost in my work
I concentrate a lot on my work	I don't feel stress
I pay a lot of attention to my work	I don't get distracted

Attention is still good – many struggle even to get that far – but absorption is wonderful. You've probably had that feeling when you're applying yourself to a hobby or other interest. It's great when you get that feeling at work too. Some commentators (including, interestingly the Dalai Lama) say that work shouldn't be about accessing a series of absorption 'events' but that we should feel this all of time. This is at best unrealistic and at worst naive. Realism is more helpful than the pursuit of perfection. The SPARC is so important for engagement and if we have it then we can deal with those times when things aren't exactly as we want them.

 **recap**

- Your effectiveness in the medium and long term will be a consequence of the level at which you engage in what you are doing.

- Be honest with yourself – how much control do you need over your job? How much are you willing to cede to others?

- Whatever you do, whenever you do it, find a reason for doing it.

- Find a good match between the treasures that lie within you and what you do when you work. Too much misalignment leads to unhappiness, ineffectiveness and perhaps even destructiveness.

- Be clear about the rewards you get from your work beyond financial remuneration

- Seek out learning opportunities that stretch you.

- Paying attention to the job is good, absorption in it is even better

Maximising personal effectiveness

There is a measure available to monitor personal effectiveness as you apply yourself to different situations. In any realm of working life there will be two variables by which you will be able to monitor how effective you will be. These are your strategy/approach and the likelihood that you will succeed. They can be worked into a simple formula:

Personal effectiveness (the goal) = Strategy x Likelihood of success

or

$$99\% = 10 \times 10$$

You score a maximum of 99 per cent because nothing is 100 per cent guaranteed even if you do everything perfectly. Right away you should recognise that how you apply this formula will be highly subjective. Nonetheless, what it does is help you think through what you need to do to maximise your effectiveness in any given situation. Its first application is its use in preparation. The second application is to use it to assess why you have/haven't been effective when you come to assess success, again in a particular situation. To that end it's a very good catalyst for reflection and learning.

So, how does it work? Quite simply each of the dimensions is given a score up to a maximum of 10. The two scores are then multiplied together to give a final score up to 99. The scoring requires application and honesty. First you need to identify in what aspect of your working life (or indeed any part of your life) you want to be effective. This could be: having a difficult conversation with a colleague; raising a very delicate issue at the next team meeting; working on a specific project; or whatever it is that occupies your thoughts at the moment. Then take the following steps:

1   Look at your strategy and assess its strength in terms of its quality and systematic thinking. Clearly the score will be

low (1–3) if your thinking has been rushed or unfocused. A higher score will occur when rigour has been applied to the development of your strategy.

2   The same scale applies to likelihood of success. Your major variable within 'likelihood of success' will be risk. In many areas of personal effectiveness, risk comes in the form of the predictability or unpredictability of human behaviour. It is this assessment of human behaviour that is so crucial in many areas of personal effectiveness. You can manage and control yourself but you can only influence others and that creates a degree of uncertainty in predicting success.

 **example**

Say you want to introduce a new idea at a meeting (a theme we look at in Chapter 7). You know that the majority of the people in the room will be resistant to your idea. This immediately reduces the likelihood of success and your score will be lower. In another situation you need to ask a favour from a colleague with whom you have a good working relationship. You know the favour will be inconvenient to your colleague but because you have done favours for your colleague in the past you think the reaction should be favourable. Although nothing should be taken for granted your likelihood of success will be that much higher. Here you are assessing your capacity to influence others (we cover this in Chapter 6).

The goal

However, you do need to decide specifically what it is you are trying to achieve – hence the reason that the word 'goal' appears next to 'personal effectiveness' in the formula. In the meeting scenario in the 'Brilliant example' above are you actually trying to get the team to say 'yes' to your idea or are you looking to secure agreement at this stage that the idea is worth looking at further? Clearly the second goal has a better chance of success than the first and you can then refine your strategy accordingly. Sometimes a 'step-by-step' approach works best – particularly when human beings and our resistance to change are concerned. (Goal-setting is covered in Chapter 4.)

A learning experience

Part of the strength of this formula is that it can be used as a learning tool. In some situations where we need to be effective we do not have the advantage of preparation time to develop a strategy. Here the formula can be applied in hindsight. You will not have the advantage of defining the goal but you can still, either through asking others or subjectively, consider how effective you were in a particular situation. You can then look back at your approach in the situation you are looking at. For example, let's take a person who receives some feedback from his manager and gets told something that he doesn't want to hear – even though the manager has a point. He reacts defensively and when that approach isn't helpful, reacts emotionally. In hindsight, realising that defensiveness and emotional responses are not helpful when receiving feedback he works through what will be a more productive approach next time.

brilliant tip

You can also reflect on your 'likelihood of success' with the added advantage of hindsight. I am sure many people, on reflection, say 'I was biting off far more than I could chew' when things don't go well. It's great to have big goals but the best way to reach them is in small steps.

Your score

Over 80 per cent

Time for a reality check. If your score is this high have another look at your strategy – have you really thought through the issues? Particularly people issues. What is the likelihood of success – is the goal a big one in which case the likelihood of success will be reduced? If, after this recheck you are sure, then your effectiveness is likely to be high.

Making a presentation is a good one to include here. It is a situation in which you can look at 'you' in great detail and have control over what you do. You must have a clear goal (e.g. 'after my presentation the team will understand the three steps they need to take to approve a new account'). You then do all the preparation needed to give yourself the best chance of success including your own 'performance'. However, every group is different and you can never discount the tough audience. What you do is maximise your chances of the audience being with you throughout the presentation.

We use delivering a presentation as a working example later (see Chapter 5).

50–80 per cent

So, your effectiveness will be lower – your goal might not be reached. Look again at your strategy. Anything you haven't thought of? Anything extra you can do to increase your likelihood of success? And critically, do you need to change your goal to make it a more realistic one?

0–49 per cent

Less than 50 per cent chance of success? As before check your strategy, check your likelihood of success and, if necessary, look again at your goal. However, it is worth bearing in mind that in many aspects of life itself we accept these odds. Ever heard the story of the marketing manager who said, 'We know 50 per cent of our marketing budget is money well-spent and 50 per cent isn't. The trouble is we don't know which 50 per cent is.'

Setbacks and failure are often prerequisites for success, if you learn from them and acknowledge that 'failing doesn't make me a failure'. So, even if the odds are low, that doesn't mean you shouldn't go ahead with something. This thinking can even be applied to managing your day.

Even though you do your planning first thing, events often come along that compromise even your best-laid plans. The unexpected request, the avalanche of emails or the unpredictable mini-crisis are all examples of things which challenge us. What we are saying here is that even though no day will ever work out exactly as you plan it you should still plan. Even though you will be disturbed, will need to answer emails and be asked to do things you hadn't planned for you can still get on with your working day in anticipation of this. Some even advocate that we plan for the unexpected. Building in the unexpected increases personal effectiveness.

 **brilliant** recap

- In any area of personal effectiveness you need to be clear what you are trying to achieve.
- This can take the form of a specific goal.
- You can maximise effectiveness by thinking through your strategy beforehand.
- You can maximise effectiveness by asking what your likelihood of success is.
- Use your experiences as learning opportunities.
- Don't underestimate the effect others have on your own personal effectiveness.
- Setbacks and failure can be good if you respond in the right way.

CHAPTER 3

Managing
yourself

'While we are postponing, life speeds by.'

Seneca, Roman philosopher

Self-organisation

Is there anything more important for personal effectiveness than how we make use of the time available to us at work? One of the great frustrations of managing time is that we want the 'perfect' solution – the simple answer that provides for maximum effectiveness. It's understandable. But the interesting part of this is that there is a perfect solution. The problem is that few people, particularly those who never seem to have enough time, want to hear the solution because deep-down they know what it is. *Self-discipline.* You either discipline yourself to plan, prioritise, organise and be assertive or you don't. You either discipline yourself to manage the times you check emails, stay off social networking websites and avoid idle chit-chat and gossip or you don't. There is no mystery here. It's just that common sense isn't always common practice.

So, now that we have slayed one particular dragon let's slay a few others.

Dragon 1 – I can multitask

'Attempting to perform several tasks at once may run into difficulties of several kinds. For example it is impossible to say two different things at exactly the same time, and it may be easier to combine an auditory and a visual task than it is to combine two visual and two auditory tasks.'

Daniel Kahneman, psychologist

Daniel Kahneman's quote reveals the difficulty of multitasking. He then says that there is some evidence that with a lot of practice we can multitask in very specific ways. What seems likely is that this practice leads to a very high level of proficiency in certain things that can be done so instinctively that you barely need to think about them because you do them so often. It's a bit like the way a highly skilled drummer/percussionist can use both hands and feet to do four different things at the same time and bring them together into a coherent 'whole'. You may recognise that feeling yourself. You can probably 'juggle' with a lot of things that are very familiar, tuning out and tuning in quickly as the day rolls along. However, throw in one or two things that are relatively unfamiliar, that require deeper application, then the juggling act becomes a lot more difficult and of course the pressure that you felt before (manageable) then becomes stressful and therefore less likely to be manageable if it's enduring.

The lesson here is to do one thing at a time to its completion wherever possible.

Dragon 2 – I can manage time

We can't manage time. Time is a finite concept. A day doesn't suddenly last 27 hours. We can't stretch it, bend it, shape it or alter it. Strangely people think they can. They get up earlier and go to bed later to fit in all the work that needs to be done. They develop bad eating habits, skip lunch, shovel in a load of sugar at around 4 p.m. to 'keep going', drink that extra glass or two of wine to 'de-stress' and wish their lives away waiting for the big summer holiday. Not managing time properly kills people. There is only one thing that can be managed and it is ourselves. So, look at managing your time as really being about managing yourself.

Dragon 3 – I have a problem that no one else has

Each life is unique but the problems within it, as far as lack of time is concerned, are not. Others share the same problems and some have worked their way round those problems and even created opportunities for themselves. Here is a story from 'Amanda' featured in my book *Make Your Own Good Fortune* which illustrates this.

brilliant example

I have a stressful job. I work full-time and have four children aged between 8 and 18. For a long-time I juggled all the balls but always lacked 'me' time. I'd get home at 5 p.m. and it was straight into the world of cooking, cleaning and so on. I knew there were plenty of other people in the world in the same position so I began to see if I there was a way to get a bit of 'me' time. I made a tough decision. When I describe it, it sounds brutal but in reality it wasn't like that at all.

I gathered my family together on the sofa and told them that after 8 p.m. is my time. I'm not cooking, cleaning, washing, ironing or doing anything else other than things for me. Suddenly I had a bit of breathing space. I could do some reading, get on the internet, some gardening in the summer which I really enjoy and generally start to reactivate my brain. Of course, what happened was that, as I stopped doing things for people then they realised quite quickly that they had to do it for themselves. I even caught my 16-year-old doing a bit of ironing. I started doing an evening class and I feel a bit liberated as a result.

▶

It hasn't reduced my effectiveness one bit. What it has done is given me an opportunity to freshen myself up - to take an opportunity to enjoy a bit of leisure time that I didn't believe existed. I think it's made me a better person at work too. I'm less grumpy and a bit more balanced. I've injected some perspective into my life.

Dragon 4 – I know what I am doing

Writer Daniel Pink (Pink, 2008) invites us to write down the things that are important to us. But, as he says, 'Does the reality of our daily lives match the rhetoric of our deepest aspirations?' The things we should write down – no more than ten – should cover people (those who are the most important to you), activities and critically, your values (you could refer to the character strengths questionnaire cited in Chapter 2 to help with this). Then, do a simple comparison between this list of ten or so items and your planner, diary, calendar or whatever you use that will tell you how you've spent the last month. How often have you accessed the truly important things? If you need an incentive to manage yourself better at work then this is it.

⟩brilliant impact

At what part of the day are you at your best? For most of us it's those critical first couple of hours of the working day. And yet this is the time when many will work through a series of relatively unimportant emails, discuss the previous evening over the coffee machine or deal with things that may be relatively enjoyable to do but don't really impact on your overall effectiveness.

Get the critical, important stuff done first thing when your mind is at its freshest and you're at your most energetic. There is an added advantage to this. No day is perfect and no matter how well you plan ahead things will come along to challenge those carefully made plans. Mini-crises, disturbances, urgent requests and overrunning meetings all compromise the best time managers. By getting the 'must-do', tough stuff done first thing you don't find yourself rushing to get it done, last thing.

Being disciplined: getting organised

At its worst, stress at work kills people. If it doesn't kill, it seriously compromises health and well-being. It's a theme we are going to look at in the second section of this chapter. One of the reasons we get stressed is because we don't discipline and organise ourselves. So, here we look at four classic 'time thieves' together with recommendations to help you think about how you manage yourself during the day.

Time thief 1: Doing first what should be last

'*There is never enough time to do everything, but there is always enough time to do the most important thing.*'

Brian Tracy, author

ABCDE is a planning technique advocated by Brian Tracy in his book *Eat That Frog* as a way of planning at the beginning of the day. There are people who advocate planning your day just before you leave work the night before. Do what works best for you. Tracy tells us to divide all the tasks that need to be done in the following way.

A Tasks – Must be done or there will be serious consequences.

B Tasks – Should get done but if not the consequences will be milder than A tasks.

C Tasks – Like to get done but no consequences if they don't get done.

D Tasks – I can delegate this. Pass on – through your manager if you can't directly delegate – the things that others can do so that you do the things only you can do.

E Tasks – I can eliminate this.

A good question that many ask is 'What do I do if I have, say, three 'A' tasks today?' You simply prioritise the A tasks: A-1, A-2, A-3 for example, and get on with A-1 right away.

Your ABCDE list is a focused version of what's known as a 'to do' list. Why not look at this another way and develop a 'to don't' list as well? Think of all the bad practices people typically have. Maybe you have some of these yourself. Here are some examples.

- I find it difficult to say 'no' to requests.
- I check my emails as soon as I get in. And then do so every five minutes for the rest of the day.
- I randomly start web-surfing and checking my social networks (e.g. looking at cat memes on Facebook).
- Doing the things I like doing least at the worst time of day (e.g. tough tasks right after lunch).
- Drifting through 'prime-time', i.e. between 9 and 11 a.m. and then rushing to complete stuff at the end of the day.
- Working (all) weekend.

brilliant tips

- Estimate the start *and* finish time for each task. Most of us think only about when we're going to start.
- Beware 'schedule creep' – things that keep getting added to the list. Adding something? Then take something else off.

Time thief 2: Email

'I'm also not going to tell you email is evil, because it isn't. The negative productivity impact of email comes from the way you use it, not the medium itself.'

Olé Eichhorn, well-known blogger

Email has some terrific benefits but it's become arguably the classic time trap in its short life.

First some reminders about what email isn't meant for.

- It is not a substitute for talking face-to-face.
- It is not meant to 'cover your back', i.e. you can't say 'I told you that last Wednesday' when in actual fact what you did was send an email.
- It is not a means of delaying decision-making.

And a reminder too of what you are not.

- You aren't paid to be a semi-skilled email typist.
- You aren't paid to be distracted every few minutes by your email. Email is a means to help you get results, not a diversion from work.

So, there are things we shouldn't be doing and what should we do?

- **You choose when you use**. Pick the moment at which you'll be interrupted – you choose when to check your email don't let it choose you. Aim for two to three blocks per day. Also, turn off any sound that accompanies the arrival of an email in your inbox. Your day-to-day effectiveness depends on this.
- **You'll be late if you debate.** Use face-to-face meetings or phone calls instead. Conversations are usually best for decision and resolution. That goes for criticism as well.

Email debate often goes 'round the houses' with people restating their own points ad infinitum. You will be late home if you end on the email treadmill.

- **You're out of line if you waste my time.** Don't waste other people's time by making them think you are busy. If you send a lot of emails (or 'cc' a lot of people) the number of emails you receive grows exponentially with an increasing lifecycle.

- **What will they think if you skimp on the ink?** Email, while it can have a less formal feel, should not be used as an excuse to give up on attention to detail. Poor spelling, abbreviations, jargon and a lack of punctuation and grammar can give an 'I can't be bothered' impression, particularly with external contacts. Use spell checkers and ask how someone reading it might react. Is this the reaction you want?

- **Once you send there is no end.** Email lasts forever. What record do you want to leave?

brilliant tip

There's currently a lot of debate about the use of 'emoticons'. Not that long ago there was an assumption that it wasn't professional to use them. Then along comes some research that seemed to show they do make a difference to mood and rapport in some online/ mobile phone workplace interactions. The jury's still out on when you use them and with whom. The best advice is let others take the lead. If they use them, and you feel comfortable using them, then use them.

Time thief 3: Procrastination

The old saying goes that 'procrastination is the thief of time'. While misuse of email runs it close most of us recognise that putting the things off that we don't like doing is one of the biggest hurdles to overcome. It's understandable. Time is always a function of priority – what's most important at that moment – and it's entirely natural that we want to prioritise the things we enjoy doing the most. As we saw earlier it is very hard to get past 'self-discipline' when it comes to getting the important things done, particularly when they may not be the things you enjoy doing. So, here are some suggestions to help you overcome the hurdle of procrastination – with a large dose of self-discipline – if it is an issue for you. And let's face it, for most of us it is.

- **Build it into the 'big' picture.** The SPARC model, and the research that created it, told us that 'purpose' – having a reason to do something – is critical for engagement and motivation. The more we can connect what we do to a higher purpose the more likely we are to be motivated to do it. If there is no compelling reason then question why you are doing it or if it's something that's been delegated to you then ask your manager.

- **Try to be accountable to someone for everything you do.** This takes the first point a step further. Sometimes that 'purpose' will be that your performance of the task makes someone else's job easier.

- **Make your work significant.** Your output and effectiveness depends on your attitude. If you believe that what you do is significant then you are likely to be more motivated to deliver.

- **Have a deadline.** There are time management purists who say that what makes any task 'important' is if it *must* be done now, i.e. the deadline has arrived. There may be things on your 'to do' list which can be shifted but the principle of having a deadline for everything is a good one. It creates a degree of pressure which compels us to get the job done.

● **Doing things for other people that extend beyond your own immediate needs is a great habit to get into.** The most effective workplaces tend to be those where shared values based on collaboration, mutuality and support are the norm. Venality might deliver quick results in the shortest of short terms but toxicity and failure will be the only outcome. Helping others meet their needs gives you the best chance of others helping you to meet yours. In all cases 'behaviour breeds behaviour'.

● **Do not disturb.** One study found that in an office environment we are disturbed by the phone, email, requests or 'office chat' on average every 15 minutes. That's not helpful if you or I need to concentrate on a piece of work for a sustained period. To get that precious hour or so needed every day for serious concentration suggest to your colleagues that you have a system where each team member gets an hour per day when other team members provide cover for the person who needs to get on with something. Alternatively, assertiveness skills may be needed (see Chapter 6) if this is a personal need for a specific project, so that you can get time to yourself in a quiet room.

Time thief 4: Interruptions

'Be ruthless with time but gracious with people.'

Anon

Plan for disturbances
Don't have your schedule planned so tightly that you have no slack for interruptions and the unexpected. If you have say, an hour of floating time, and it doesn't get filled with the unexpected then that's a bonus but it's likely to be rare. So, be realistic when planning. Some jobs are predominantly reactive (certain kinds of

call centre work, for example) so the day is always like this, but most jobs aren't. Managing interruptions is inevitable.

What's the new priority?

When interrupted you need to look again at priorities. If it's your manager making a request you know that he or she has the ultimate say in what your priorities are. You may disagree – in which case the assertiveness skills covered later (in Chapter 6) will be applicable. The manager's request is likely to become the new priority unless the deadline is some time away. In the 'Brilliant example' below we look at a way in which you can deal with a request that comes late in the day from your manager. It contains many of the essences of good time management practice.

brilliant example

It's late in the afternoon. You need to get away on time as you have a commitment after work that's important to you. You've managed to get almost everything done on your 'to do' list. Just a couple of things left and just enough time to do them. At this point your manager approaches and asks 'Can you do this by the end of the day?' It's not particularly convenient and you can't just directly say 'no'. So what do you do? There are options.

● You need to establish specifically what the request is and the estimated time it will take. You also need to understand the real deadline – people are very good at saying 'by the end of the day' when they don't actually need it for a couple of days. It seems to be an insurance against the fear of only having work delivered back at the very last moment. 'As soon as possible' is never good enough.

● This isn't your problem. It's your manager's problem and the manager has decided to pass it on to you. So, reflect the problem back with the use of the constructive 'no'. State your workload clearly to your manager and then ask an assumptive question: 'I have these tasks to complete by the end of the day. Which of them would you like to me leave until tomorrow so that I get your request done on time?'

▶

- You are likely to get one of several possible responses. 'OK, it can be left until tomorrow, I don't need it until lunchtime.' Or 'OK, I will see if I can get Sam to do it while you get on with what's left.' Or 'I think we can leave that until tomorrow, does this leave you with enough time to get on with my request?'

Of course, not everything is so straightforward and situations like this don't always play out so easily but the technique of reflecting the problem back and being helpful, even accommodating at the same time, is a sound one. There are times when we have to accommodate, and if you want your career to progress, this will be essential. But if all you do is accommodate others all that happens is that you get used. You are the person who always says 'yes'.

Language, paralanguage, body language

Your reaction to interruptions will determine how long the interruption lasts for. You can keep it short. It's a good idea to stand up or perch on the edge of your desk when interrupted. Something other than the posture you adopted before the interruption. This sends out a signal that you are 'on the move', i.e. busy, and that you want the interruption to be brief. It's also good practice to make sure there isn't a second chair available to use – you don't want the interrupter to get too cosy. Paralanguage – which refers to the way words come out – should be friendly, professional and assertive.

Finally, think about the impact of the words you use. When asked a question such as 'Have you got a minute?' avoid saying 'Yes'. It's open-ended and may even imply that you are not busy. Better to say something along the lines of 'I have five minutes' which implies a degree of accommodation but within a limit. Of course, when interrupted with a request there are two things you need to know: 'What are you asking me to do?' and 'When do you want it by?'

The type of interruption

Interruptions maybe related to work requests but they can just as easily be unrelated to work. Office discussions go on all the time and we know from studies about why people come to work – aside from money – that a social environment is important for some of them. Time management perfectionists might say don't get involved, but life isn't quite so simple. You don't want to be disconnected from the subtleties and nuances of everyday office life. So much information gets passed around through informal networks and the grapevine that doesn't travel through formal communication systems. It's about learning when to tune into what's being discussed and when to tune out.

 **impact**

In his seminal works on differences between people, academic and culture expert Fons Trompenaars talks of the way in which some people need to feel that strong relationships that permeate beyond the confines of the workplace are a natural part of working life. While some see working relationships as purely professional, not extending into any area beyond what is required to 'get the job done', others want to 'get to know you' and for you 'to get to know them'. You probably know people at work whom you don't know anything about beyond the working environment, while with others you seem to know the minutiae of their whole lives. There is no judgement to be made here. What is important is that for long-term effectiveness at work you will need to master the skills of influencing, persuasion and negotiation. Your trustworthiness and credibility are so important here and with some people you get this by being part of their lives so that even if you are not actively involved in it they know that you understand it. You need to invest time in the relationship and that will eat into some of your time. It can be an investment that reaps dividends.

Who's interrupting?

Are the same people interrupting you? Do certain people seem to be making requests at certain times of the day, i.e. towards the end of the day? Is this indicative of their own disorganisation and therefore by extension their disorganisation affects your organisation?

If there is a pattern to this you will need to approach the person concerned. Later (in Chapter 6) we look at the skill of 'mental rehearsal' as a means of preparing ourselves for difficult conversations.

brilliant tip

Over time people start to pick up on the patterns of behaviour of others. Earlier in this section we looked at an example of this when if you are the person who always says 'yes' to requests you become the person everyone goes to with requests. The two aspects feed each other. If you can get into the habit of going to people rather than them coming to you - particularly with persistent interrupters - over time the pattern of behaviour gets noticed.

brilliant recap

- It starts with a word - self-discipline.
- Do one thing at a time to completion - mono-task.
- Be creative in the way you create free time.
- Use ABCDE for planning and prioritising tasks.
- Email - choose when you use, don't be an email slave.
- Time is a function of priority - be clear on what your priorities are at any given time.
- Disturbances are inevitable, the consequences are not.

Renewing your energy levels

'A healthy body is a guest-chamber for the soul; a sick body is a prison.'

Francis Bacon, polymath

We ask a lot of ourselves professionally – particularly those of us for whom professional success is important and even more so by those who define themselves by what they do and have done professionally. But with these demands comes the potential for physical and emotional damage and it's the aim of this, the second section of this chapter to:

- look at the dangers of taking too much energy out of yourself without having a means of refreshment and renewal, and

- suggest ways in which this 'refreshment and renewal' can happen.

You probably aren't reading this book because of some sort of vague, abstract interest in the subject of personal effectiveness. It may well be because you are striving to get better, to increase your performance standards and take your career to the next level. It's definitely a good thing too. But how often do you check in with yourself – really ask yourself how you are feeling physically and emotionally? Are you taking too much out without putting enough back in? We know what the damage can be to health if we use our bodies and minds like bank accounts where we are withdrawing cash but not keeping the balance in the bank account in a healthy state, not replacing what we've used. We also know that that this failure to keep the account in credit, or at least in a balanced state, will fundamentally affect performance. No one performs at their best when the physical and mental account is always in overdraft. Some of us as, the 'Brilliant quote' below says, flog ourselves even when we know the damage we are doing.

'How sick can you get and still come to work?'

C. W. Metcalf, author and stress management expert

Brilliant performance

In his book *Be Excellent at Anything* (co-authored with Jean Gomes and Caroline McCarthy) Tony Schwartz presents a valuable model which helps us to describe how we are feeling at work and how beneficial or destructive those feelings are. Before going through this model it is useful to write down a few words to describe how you feel. As this book concentrates more on work use 'work' adjectives to describe how you feel at work. Try to come up with five or six single words rather than sentences.

You are now in a position to do a well-being audit. Have a look at the four quadrants below. Each quadrant is a zone which describes a state of being. Each zone connects 'feelings' with 'energy' – for example the 'performance zone' being a zone where energy is high and feelings are positive.

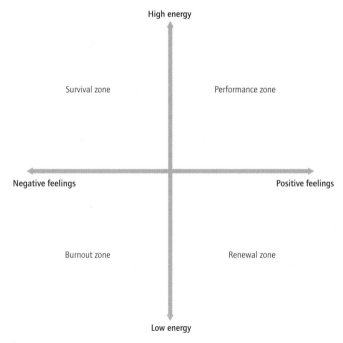

Schwartz encourages us to tune into our own emotions – using our emotional intelligence – what we're thinking, how we are feeling and what our current energy levels are. You will see below some of the words we associate with these zones. As you work through the zones consider the words that you have used to describe your current state and ask which zone they best fit into.

Burnout zone: Low energy, Negative feelings

We associate these words with this state: exhausted, empty, depressed, sad, hopeless

Survival zone: Higher energy, Negative feelings

We associate these words with this state: impatient, irritable, frustrated, angry, defensive, fearful, anxious, worried

Renewal zone: Low energy, Positive feelings

We associate these words with this state: carefree, peaceful, relieved, mellow, receptive

Performance zone: High energy, Positive feelings

We associate these words with this state: calm, optimistic, challenged, engaged, invigorated

At one time or another we've all experienced the 'performance' zone – when we're deeply connected with what we are doing and operating at an optimal level. We are also unstressed. The 'challenge' we feel creates a degree of positive pressure that fuels us rather than diminishes. So, here's the next question. Although we've all experienced the 'performance zone' we don't experience it all of the time. Where do we go? The dangers of being in the burnout zone for too long are well-established and those associated emotions such as 'empty' and 'hopeless' will do us great psychological and physical damage if we stay there too long.

Aware of this danger, and of the difficulty of accessing the performance zone, many revert to the survival zone. Some of us opt for the survival zone because we find it hard to say 'I feel depressed' or 'I'm exhausted' at work so we choose to 'hide' what we're really thinking and feeling. Of course many of the emotions connected with the survival zone 'leak' out even if we try to conceal them. You can only be irritable and anxious for so long and successfully hide it.

Perhaps the zone that is utilised the least is the renewal zone. Even those operating consistently in the 'performance zone' need to refresh, recalibrate and restore energy levels so that when we return to performing we are at our best.

Renewal

'If fitness is described as the speed of recovery physically then resilience is the speed of recovery emotionally.'

Tony Schwartz, author and founder of 'The Energy Project'

Optimal performance requires us to take a step back from performing if those high-performance levels are to be sustainable. To be consistently effective at work you need to know when and how to replenish – even when you are performing well and feeling unstressed. We have already looked at some of the symptoms that reveal themselves when we are in the burnout or survival zones. These symptoms are clear indicators that that a move to the renewal zone is needed. It's pointless continuing to perform when there is little energy to draw on and few positive emotions about yourself and the work you are doing. In this section we look at how we can replenish ourselves – building up our energy stores and reinforcing positive emotions.

Connect and disconnect

Many of us find it hard to truly connect with what we're doing and to truly disconnect. Instead we operate in a state of partial connection where we start on something, get distracted by something else (or bored with what we're doing) and then make a start on that before the same thing happens. Similarly when we're supposed to be disconnected, i.e. not at work or 'working', with family or friends, at 'play' (hobbies, etc.) or even on holiday, we are inclined to partially connect. We tend to check emails (and send them) when it's rest time or 'half-think' about work when we don't need to be thinking about it all.

Top sports performers are used to training and performing with high intensity and know the value of total rest and replenishment afterwards before the time comes for the next burst of sustained performance. One feeds the other. Optimum performance comes with a clear strategy for optimal renewal. It starts with truly switching off for a time, from what it is that demands your best performance.

 **example**

In the Bibliography you will find a YouTube link featuring tennis player and Wimbledon champion Marion Bartoli as she goes through a rigorous practice session. She has various pieces of elastic attached to her arms and legs, pulling against her natural direction of movement to simulate the moments in a match when she is very tired and finds it a struggle to move her muscles. Her coach throws balls at her in very quick succession and she has to return them. It's incredibly intense. But it's also not something she does for hours. She, and other professionals, practise intensely (their version of our 'learning'), perform intensely and then restore themselves to equilibrium. Marion Bartoli talked about how much better 'rested' she was for the 2013 Wimbledon (which she won) compared to the 2007 final (which she lost). Brilliant effort needs the right counterweight of rest and renewal.

Filling the vacuum

Viktor Frankl was one of the great twentieth-century psycho-therapists. He argued that a primary driver in our lives is creating meaning for ourselves. Work that we enjoy, interests, strong relationships, spiritual fulfilment and our family can create meaning. But, through misalignment (perhaps we have a job that doesn't resonate at all), or a lack of an outlet to truly express ourselves (a hobby or interest) some start to develop an existential vacuum. Frankl describes it as the blocking of the spirit.

If there is something to fill a vacuum it will, inevitably, fill it. In the same way, if we have this existential vacuum, we too look to fill it. What do we fill the vacuum with?

What are the touchstones that help you to reconnect with the real 'you'? What do you enjoy doing? Can you recall things that you have really enjoyed doing, that challenged you? Getting bogged down can mean forgetting or even losing your touchstones. Domestic circumstances and other things can flip you into 'what I can't do' mode rather than the more positive 'what I can do' mind-set that sparks energising thoughts.

▶ brilliant example

Here's something to consider. Do you have people around you offering you free advice about what you should and shouldn't do? The advice is often given with the best of intentions but with little consideration for the real you. What most people do is advise you to do what suits them. So if you've ever heard advice along the lines of 'You should take up tennis' or 'Yoga would be good for you' or 'Why don't you try jogging?' you will have experienced this at first-hand. This is the point where you must think of the real you. What's going to give you renewal is what connects with you most deeply – as we said before, your 'catalysts'. The catalysts are the things that draw you to them rather than the things that you have to force yourself to be drawn to. It might be a physical thing (for this writer it's the pleasure of being in a pool, three times a week, for 40 minutes intense swimming). It could be some form of mental stimulation. It could also be doing absolutely nothing and enjoying it!

If you give children time and space and switch the gadgets off they might sit in a chair saying 'I'm bored' for a bit. But eventually then they go off and do something – particularly if you really do put the gadgets away. Observe a child who loves to paint, draw and create. Observe another who sets up a classroom in her bedroom and teaches her teddy bears whatever she's learned at school most recently. These are both real examples. That something provides a window into what it is that truly connects the way they occupy themselves with the treasures that lie deepest within them – and possibly also a window into what they could be doing when they start work if they are to be happy.

So, the question for you is 'What is your deepest inner treasure?' – the catalysts and resources within you that allow you to express yourself to the world and be 'you'. The things that give your life true meaning rather than the things that get thrown into the existential vacuum.

First-time experiences

One of the contributors to burnout and survival is repetition. We have to be realistic. Not all jobs offer a conveyor belt of new and varied opportunities each day. But, as curious, intelligent, inventive people variety in a job, as in life, is important. If the job doesn't give new experiences then we need to find them in other parts of life. With stagnation a possibility – and potentially a destructive one – the search for new first-time experiences provides a counterweight to this. A good catalysing question to ask is 'When was the last time you did something for the first time?'

It is said that life speeds up as you get older. Experts in memory say that one of the reasons for this is because we have fewer first-time experiences and it's the first-time experiences in life that are truly memorable. If you're young and reading this, keep those new experiences rolling in – in the job and beyond it if you can. If you are older don't neglect the invigorating effects of doing something new. Avoid 'stuckness'.

Sensory stimulation

Did you ever get that 'feeling of being alive'? Think for a moment about this, where it last happened and in particular when it last happened. Some people get this from the rigour of sporting activity (combined with the lovely feeling of hormonal release, post-exercise, that makes us feel mellow). Others from a great holiday, a long walk or stimulating company. There are also other more subtle ways we can reconnect and they relate to the way you stimulate your senses. These can be simple things and in isolation they won't deliver complete renewal. But as a counterweight to the demands of peak performance they make a significant contribution to our need for renewal.

Here is something for you to try if you think that conscious sensory stimulation can make a difference to you. The first is to think of the most recent occasions you can recall your senses being stimulated. Below you will find some ideas to trigger your thinking. Perhaps those 'last time' experiences aren't so recent? Next to this is an opportunity to write down where and when you might stimulate those five senses in the near future.

Sense	The last time?	The next time?
Taste	————————	————————
Touch	————————	————————
Sight	————————	————————
Smell	————————	————————
Hearing	————————	————————

To stimulate your thoughts here are some suggestions.

Taste: good wine; home-cooked food; a glass of ice-cold water when you're hot and thirsty.

Touch: love-making; soil; skin; food; wood; plants; water; animal fur.

Sight: the highest point in your town; going to the cinema; a new place each week no matter how local; art; football match; the night sky.

Hearing: music; real silence; ambient sounds; sports crowds; libraries.

Smell: the countryside; a forest after the rain; fresh coffee; the sea.

In the moment

What makes us effective at work – getting the task completed, moving on to the next one – can permeate our lives outside the workplace and even during those times when we take a break at work. By moving from one thing to the next we fail to appreciate what's immediately around us. Life speeds past. So, what does this mean in practice? It means that we should also consciously connect with the moment. When eating it means actually savouring the taste of the food, drawing breath and taking time to enjoy it, rather than seeing it as means of refuelling before moving quickly on to the next thing. Eating lunch at your desk while working is one of the worst manifestations of this. When out, it means taking in what's around you – when walking down the street when was the last time you averted your gaze from eye level and looked up? When reading, avoid doing three other things at the same time and just concentrate on the beauty of the words. It's about being truly present in the moment.

An extension of this is to pay close attention to your thoughts, feelings and sensations while you're doing whatever it is you're doing. This is a part of what's been labelled 'mindfulness' over the past few years although it's been accepted practice within, for example, parts of Buddhism for a long time.

What's around you?

This is an extension of the 'in the moment' idea above. Many of us look forward to a holiday. Some of us start looking forward to a holiday as soon as the last one has ended. Having things to look forward to is great but by doing so we may be bypassing what's actually around us, accessible and free. It's about avoiding the association with home as 'work', i.e. somewhere I get to work from, and the association with holiday as 'play'. Of course we take the odd day off but that's often used for catching up with chores, trips to the dentist and other routine domestic tasks. So, the suggestion here is not just to see a day or two off work as a 'day off' but rather a 'holiday at home'. Try being a tourist where you live and you see things that you normally take for granted. Feel positive about your local surroundings and remind yourself that there are great opportunities for renewal on your doorstep.

Something for you

While doing things for and with others brings reward there should be a little bit of space – in the 'margin' of your day – where you do one thing purely for yourself.

The positive psychologist Martin Seligman recommends that, just before bed, we recall three things that have made us happy during the day. These can be three very simple pleasures such as a conversation with an old friend, eating a particularly delicious piece of fruit, a great view or a resonating piece of music. Anything you like.

 **recap**

- The energy you take from yourself needs to be replaced. Not doing so causes stress, burnout and ill health.

- Check in with your feelings so you detect the warning signs.

- The warning signs direct you to the need for renewal.

- Some people 'hide' in the survival zone without recognising the long-term damage being done.

- Great performance comes from the ability to truly connect with what you are doing and then to truly disconnect and renew yourself.

- Know your catalysts – the things you can easily access that relax you and give you pleasure.

- Enjoy 'being in the moment' and the simple pleasures that exist around you.

CHAPTER 4

Goal achievement

'When our memories outweigh our dreams, we have grown old.'

Bill Clinton, former US president

A goal is an expression of future success that you can rationally and emotionally identify with. The goal always contains a representation of an opportunity achieved or a problem solved. In other words, 'What does success look like?' The opportunities and problems may be shared between you and a wider group or they might be personal to you.

This chapter covers the three interconnected areas of creating opportunities, solving problems and setting goals. The goal-setting element is then further split into two areas – goals and timelines. A further area also 'sit's on top of the whole chapter – that a life which consists of only the rigidly planned exploitation of opportunities and goal achievement runs the danger of being a dull one. There must be scope for surprise, captured moments of spontaneity and improvisation.

So, what's the link with personal effectiveness? You are judged by results over time. Having goals and achieving them delivers results.

Opportunities and goals

Do, be, have

Let's start, with a very big question that will challenge you to clarify your thinking around your goals. I would encourage you to think about the three questions below before you read on so that your initial thoughts at least are uncontaminated. The question comes in three parts:

- What do you want to 'BE'?
- What do you want to 'DO'?
- What do you want to 'HAVE'?

Don't restrict the time limit you put on these three questions or the scope. Don't edit your thinking either because the way you answer these questions will be instructive. There is space here to fill in your responses.

DO

BE

HAVE

So how did you respond? Some people will look at the word 'Have' and answer it materially – money, possessions and so on. Others might look at the word in a very different way. Good friendships, happy family life and health are natural responses. Others might answer 'Be' materially as in 'be rich', and 'health' can also fit here.

In my experience a majority of those over the age of 25 answer the 'Do' question as a career question, the 'Be' question as a personality/behaviour question, i.e. state of 'being', and the 'have' question materially. However, a substantial number do not.

What you are doing here is sharpening your senses so that you get a considered indication of what is important to you. No time limit was imposed on your thinking so you may have picked a point a long way into the future and answered the questions from that perspective.

Some people like to see their lives as a 'whole' and want the bigger life goals to drive them on. Perhaps you didn't do this at all because you prefer to look into the near future – towards the horizon but not over it. As far as scope is concerned you may have written down big things – 'be the CEO/MD of my current employer by the age of 40'. You may have written down something on a smaller – but perhaps no less significant to you – scale such as 'delivering my next presentation better than I delivered the last one (probably as a 'Do'). If you have had a very positive or particularly dispiriting experience recently, this will be at the forefront of your mind and may therefore be particularly important to you.

The next step is to take two or three ideas from your 'Do, Be, Have' list ('DBH') and think through their viability for you personally. Do not include anything for which only chance will determine its attainment (e.g. winning the lottery). You can place the ideas in one of the following two categories.

DBH 1 – It will never happen, e.g. trips to the outer solar
    system, winning marathons in old age, chance occurrences.

DBH 2 – It can happen.

Discount DBH1 and then progress DBH2 ideas through the following.

DBH 3 – Can happen but unlikely.

DBH 4 – Can happen and realistic.

Discount DBH 3 ideas (but don't discard entirely) and then progress DBH 4 through one of the following.

DBH 5 – I'd like it to happen.

DBH 6 – I want it to happen.

DBH 7 – It must happen.

DBH 5, DBH 6 and DBH 7 prioritises your goals. Your priority will be those in the DBH 7 category – the things you must do. These 'must happens' include job-specific essentials without which you cannot do your job properly, skills you need to develop and making your priorities at work connected with the priorities of the team, department and the organisation you work for. But the musts might also include what are known as 'itches that I need to scratch'. As we saw in Chapter 1, these are the things we love to do that call us to them rather than us having to push ourselves towards them and around which we can quite reasonably organise a big part of our lives. Then there is one more category.

DBH 8 – I'll make it happen.

Those that have made it through to this final category will present you with a big test. Having things as priorities does not necessarily make them things that engage you but if they are 'musts' you need to get through them. So, how can you do this? Quite simply by balancing the necessities (some of which will be things you really want to do anyway) with the things that feed the deepest parts of you. The 'itches that need to be scratched' truly engage and these should never be lost in the other priorities.

At the moment 'musts' that you are going to 'make happen' may be vague notions or ideas. Further on in this chapter we look at how to develop these 'musts' into tangible goals that appeal to both the rational 'head' and the emotional 'heart' in you.

brilliant tip

During your career your priorities will change – your 'Do, Be, Haves'
will change. You will decide to change jobs within your industry or
you may decide to fundamentally change what you do (I have met
several primary school teachers who are ex-lawyers). When you move
on, do so for the best of reasons. Rather than escaping from the
past move on to where the future excites you.

Being primed

'Desire sharpens the imagination and brings the event.'

Douwe Draaisma, author of *Why Life Speeds Up As You
Get Older*

Have you noticed that once you have been to a particular
country, perhaps on holiday or business, your ears prick up for
a long while after – perhaps for life – when you hear the place
mentioned on the TV, internet or radio? The same thing happens
when you buy a new car. That brand of car suddenly appears
everywhere. The point is that you have been 'primed' or 'sen-
sitised' so that you now continually notice that which you have
been exposed to. One of the advantages of 'Do, Be, Have' is that
you have now primed yourself to notice those things that give life
to your opportunity goal.

Serendipity is 'a happy accident' or a fortuitous coincidence.
But some of those 'happy accidents' are not so accidental.
Because you have now primed your mind, serendipity kicks in.
All sorts of things happen to support your opportunity. They
may well have happened anyway but you just wouldn't have
noticed them.

Have a day, at work, when you take every opportunity that you come across, no matter how trivial. An opportunity to go for lunch with a colleague; to help out in area you weren't previously involved with; to go to a meeting that's not in your core area of work; to go for a drink with a colleague after work; to listen to a problem someone has where you might have 'switched off' before... and so on. See the opportunity through. See it where it takes you.

Unstuck

In the Bibliography there is a link to a YouTube video clip. In this clip you will see two teams of basketball players – one team is dressed in white and the other black. The objective of the exercise is to count the number of times a ball is passed by the players in white. If you have access to the internet right now you will enjoy watching the clip before you read on.

The interesting part of this activity lies in what you do and don't notice. Most people get the number of passes between players in white correct. What they don't notice is the moonwalking bear that moves across the screen as the ball is being passed. They were so fixated on counting passes that they miss everything else. How about you? As the voiceover on the clip says 'It's easy to miss what you're not looking for.' This has big implications for going after a big goal. The rigidly planned pursuit of a goal, the big opportunity, may blind us to all of the other things that are going on around us.

▶ brilliant example

At a Metro station in Washington DC a busker played six Bach pieces on the violin totalling 45 minutes during the rush hour. It's estimated that 1,100 people went past him during that time. Six actually stopped to listen. The one who stopped the longest was the youngest – a boy approximately three years old – until his mother moved him on. Twenty people gave money but did so while continuing to walk. He collected $32. He finished playing and a young lady engaged him in a brief conversation.

Two nights before the violinist had been playing a sold out concert in Boston where the seats cost over $100. The violinists name? Joshua Bell. One of the greatest musicians in the world had just played one of the hardest pieces to perform.

In an unusual setting and at a strange time people were not able to grasp the opportunity to hear a great musician perform for free. What are you missing because it is not convenient or the circumstances aren't right?

And the young lady who was talking to him at the end? She had seen him in concert and she knew who he was. She had been 'primed'.

Are you curious enough?

'The creation of something is not accomplished by the intellect but by the play instinct arising from inner necessity. The creative mind plays with the object it loves.'

Carl Jung, psychiatrist and psychotherapist

Opportunity spotting is just another form of creativity. And creativity requires curiosity. Curiosity is the fuel of the opportunity spotter. So, what makes us curious? Opportunity spotters are curious about themselves and their capabilities. Opportunity spotters are curious about the world beyond their own internal world. So how many of these can you tick off?

Challenge: Opportunity spotters want to test themselves. They like a bit of 'stretch' – in fact the challenge is essential. If it's not there they go out and find it.

Childlike: Children find the reasons to do things before they find reasons not to. Lots of us lose this in the move to adulthood because of lack of time, setbacks and creeping pessimism. Opportunity spotters look for the possibilities first before the pitfalls.

Confusion: If you're not confused you're not thinking clearly. Enjoy ambiguity – we don't live in a black and white world.

Creation: Do you keep yourself open to new ways of seeing and doing things?

Capture: Do you record your Eureka moments? Those 3 a.m. thoughts or the sudden arrival of a fresh idea in the bath? Opportunity spotters take those thoughts seriously. They record them too. Many of the best entrepreneurs, intrapreneurs, thinkers, writers – indeed many of those who take their random thoughts seriously – carry a notebook or an electronic device with them to make sure nothing is lost.

Comedy: Opportunity spotters are humoured and entertained by the new and intriguing. Others feel threatened.

brilliant tip

You have great value to an employer if you can ask some real opportunity-identifying questions like these.

How can we do this quicker? How can we do this cheaper? How can we do this better?

'What's currently annoying our customers about us that we can change right now?'

Alternatively, a big question that can change everything.

'What's impossible to do now, but if it could be done would fundamentally change the way we operate?' Then ask if it is actually as impossible as you think it is.

Problem-solving goals

We spend so much of our work time solving problems – sometimes they aren't even our own. Take a look at your meeting agenda at work and see how many of the agenda issues relate to problems. A good team will see these problems as opportunities – the opportunity to do something better, cheaper, quicker, more simply. Aside from the team itself you will have your own personal challenges and they are the focus of this section. Perhaps there's someone you don't get on with or you find 'difficult' and it is proving to be a barrier in getting your job done effectively. Maybe you struggle with a particular aspect of your job role and it's reducing your effectiveness. What we know is that problem definition and the setting of a goal to solve the problem requires an holistic look at the situation so that the goal you set is the right one for solving the problem itself. The way you define a problem is likely to make it so much easier to come up with the right answer.

Problem types

Take a look at the agenda items for your next team or department meeting. How many of them relate to current problems? Quite possibly the majority. We problem-solve all the time at work. Sometimes we do it collaboratively (in which case refer to Chapter 7). Quite often we solve problems on our own or with just a bit of help. This section will help you personally to define a problem accurately and then set a problem-solving goal that will solve the right problem. For you personally there are likely to be two main types of problem – cognitive problems and cooperative problems. There are others such as coordination problems though they will almost certainly be based on the organisation of a group of mostly willing people.

 brilliant definition

Cognitive problems are those where there are a single or limited number of potential solutions. An example is, 'How much of X product are we going to sell next year?' or 'How long are we going to need for the meeting now three extra people have requested to speak?'

Cooperation problems are those where individuals have their own personal agendas which make your life difficult. An example might include the classic one of dealing with what you consider to be a difficult or awkward person.

Is there a problem?

The first thing you need to do is establish if there is a problem and this means gathering evidence and drilling down into what the problem is. We shall use here two typical problems that many people will identify with in the workplace.

- **Problem 1:** 'I have difficulties getting on with a colleague when I make requests. I find him awkward.'
- **Problem 2:** 'I am finding that decisions are being taken that affect me and my work and I have little say in the decision-making process.' (You will find the 'Influencing' section within Chapter 6 has advice on dealing with this problem.)

What we now do is reduce the effect of subjectivity in assessing whether or not there is a problem by looking at the evidence.

Our assessment of the problem needs to be as objective as possible though it is entirely reasonable that a degree of gut feeling will have kicked in. Sometimes of course the evidence is instantly compelling, such as an aggressive colleague. Your evidence might include the following.

- **Problem 1:** Unproductive conversation; arguments; doesn't meet deadlines that affect you; commits to things and then does nothing; confrontational in meetings; negative body language.
- **Problem 2:** Being 'told' rather than 'consulted'; your job is to be reactive rather than proactive; not being asked to meetings when others are; comments from your own team members.

To help you assess if there is a problem use some or all of the following for evidence gathering.

- You have a specific standard and it's not being met.
- Previous experience – what's happened before isn't happening this time.
- More than one person is saying there's a problem (beware the 'sample of one').
- Statistics – bar charts, Pareto analysis, histograms, etc. are great for comparative analysis and in some instances for seeing in visual terms if a potential problem exists.
- Behaviour in others that makes you feel uncomfortable.
- Complaints.
- Gut feeling – though you might not be taken seriously if you say there's a problem to someone else and when asked 'How do you know?' you say 'It just feels like it'.

Gathering evidence is so important. A lack of evidence will reflect back to you in later steps. Say, with reference to problem 1 that you decide to talk to the colleague you find 'awkward'.

Without any specific examples you won't get very far. It's so much better to say 'When you folded your arms and raised your voice at last week's meeting it made me feel…' rather than in response to 'Why do you say I'm awkward?' you say 'Well I just think that you are'. Evidence gathering is part of the process of 'mental rehearsal' which we cover later (in Chapter 6).

brilliant tip

It's easy to fall into the trap of creating false or 'fools' problems. We say 'fools' problems because many organisations have people who live in 'fire-fighting' mode. The minor irritant becomes the catastrophe and creates the busy 'fool'. You probably know one or two of these.

Here's a more obvious example. You have a large product range and you notice a few products have been selling less well recently. If you think it is a problem you might decide to increase your marketing spend to boost sales. But these products could be past their viability in the marketplace and any sales at all are a bonus. Just because something isn't as you want it doesn't always mean it is a problem. Or in this case the problem 'goal' that you end up creating isn't:

How do we boost the sales of flagging products?

But rather:

What products can we create to replace the products that are at the end of their market viability?

So, we have a problem, we have evidence to support our view that it is indeed a problem and now we need to phrase the problem in a way that creates an effective problem-solving goal.

The problem-solving goal

One challenge for you is not to let blame cloud your definition of the problem. For example in problem 2 we see someone who finds that decisions are made that affect him or her, but he or she has little say. It's easy to point the finger at the decision-makers and say 'they have a problem'. But what if that finger pointed back at you and the decision-maker said, 'OK, it's actually your problem, how can you rethink your perspective on the problem?' You might therefore reframe the problem-solving goal to say:

How can I have more influence over the decision-making process?

It's not a problem for them (at least not one they are currently aware of) but it is for you and you need to state the problem in a way that activates you. Look at the difference between the above problem goal statement and an alternative such as: 'Stopping people taking decisions without consulting me.' The new problem goal above is no longer phrased in a way that deflates. It has an aspirational, motivating edge to it. It's become an opportunity and therefore this technique of defining the problem and refining the goal applies equally to the opportunity goals we looked at in the last section. This isn't always possible, but try to keep your problem-solving and opportunity-taking goal statements as positive as you can.

There is likely to be a pattern to the evidence that may lead you to further refine your goal. Perhaps you think not being consulted is a credibility issue, i.e. the decision-makers don't think you have sufficient credibility to be part of the decision-making process. You may develop the problem-solving goal further:

How can I build my credibility so that I have more influence in the decision-making process?

Challenge your assumptions about the problem

If we refer back to problem 2 – the 'awkward' person – you might make the assumption that the *other* person is the one who has a problem. But when you look at the problem you might find that this person's behaviour is fine with others. It's only you with whom he or she displays what you see as awkward behaviour. Your definition of the problem-solving goal will be very different if the real evidence shows something different from what you imagined it to be.

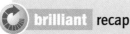 **recap**

- Analyse the evidence objectively so that you can accurately define the problem.
- Clearly state what the problem is (and what the problem isn't) based on the evidence.
- Solve the *right* problem not the easiest problem to solve.
- Refine the problem if necessary so that it accurately reflects what the problem is.
- Define a problem-solving goal that is accurate and simultaneously inspires.
- Problem-solving goals should, wherever possible, be stated as opportunities.

Setting goals

Head and heart

All goals should be checked for 'rightness' – are we sufficiently engaged with the goal rationally and emotionally so that we put the necessary work in to achieve it? We have two filters that we use to check this rightness – the rational 'head' and the emotional 'heart'. The head filter is SMART, the acronym originally conceived in the 1950s by Peter Drucker and much developed since. SMART ensures that you have coolly and rationally framed the goal in such a way as to give yourself the best chance of success. The heart filter we have already come across in this book. It is the acronym SPARC, an acronym for a process designed to ensure that you are truly emotionally engaged in what it is you want to achieve.

Putting the 'head' to work

S for specific

Goal-setting is the art of taking 'must-do's', thoughts and ideas and even seemingly impossible-to-achieve dreams and turning them into tangible, realisable statements of achievement realities. But to do this we must be specific about what we want to achieve. So much better to have a goal that says, 'we will reduce customer complaints by 75 per cent over the next 12 months' than one that says more simply 'to reduce complaints'.

M for measurable

The above contains a measure and the value of a measure is that it allows for an objective analysis of success rather than a subjective one. It is not for nothing that it is said that 'what gets measured gets done.' Most goals need intermediate measures or timelines to monitor the journey to achievement as we go. 'Timelines' are covered in the next section. There are things that just can't be measured objectively. A change in attitude is hard to measure though we can assess the impact that the change has had on our lives.

A for action-based

There's a big difference between thinking positively about something and acting positively so your goal should use active words. Passive words and phrases like 'possibly', 'try to' and 'think about' are to be avoided. Use active words such as 'create', 'increase', 'decrease' and 'succeed'.

 **example**

This is an example of what not to do. There has been some interesting new language that has appeared within political circles in the past few years – used by civil servants and politicians to reassure us that they are actively doing something. An example is the appearance of the words 'working towards' as in 'working towards a better future' or 'working towards the provision of better childcare services'. It's the way in which words can be manipulated to imply action when in fact they can just as easily mean doing nothing; there's no commitment at all. It's a slogan not a sentence with meaning. I am going to 'work towards my promotion' doesn't mean anything unless you put active words and specific measures in place.

This is an example of the management-speak that pervades the workplace. If you want to stand out as having a mind of your own *and* have impact avoid the neutering jargon that everyone else uses – 'singing from the same hymn-sheet', 'going forward' and 'best practice' are examples of what to avoid. Keep your language active, refreshing and meaningful.

R for realistic

Can you see yourself achieving this? If you can't it remains fantasy. Will the setting of effective timelines make this achievable? Can you therefore turn fantasy into reality by considering what you can do in the meantime to make the goal achievable? Are you better off having a series of relatively short-term goals? It's worth recalling that neither Bill Gates nor Steve Jobs set out to establish the giants that Microsoft and Apple have become. They had small goals that got bigger over time. Scaling down to what remains motivating (see SPARC) and realistic is healthy. If your goal remains so far over the horizon that you can't see it, then it's unlikely to drive you.

T for timed

How long is it going to take you to achieve this? 'Soon' is no good. 'Three months' is good.

Feeling with the 'heart'

One factor with SMART historically is that it technically ticks the boxes – it answers the rational thinking part of us. That's a very good start. But we are creatures of heart as well as head and we need to be truly engaged in what we do. So we need to tick the emotional boxes as well. SPARC does this and so it is the second filter through which you assess your goal. The SPARC acronym was introduced earlier (in Chapter 1) to help you understand what it is that leads to true engagement at work. Here we apply it specifically to achieving goals.

S for self-determined

You're much more likely to go for something, *and* achieve it, if you have control over the process over time. The more of a say you have over 'Who' (I work with/helps and supports me), 'How' (I go about achieving my goal), 'What' (actions I undertake to achieve my goal) and 'When' (I undertake those actions) then the more engaged you will be in your goal. Life isn't perfect – you will never have complete control – but where you don't, acknowledge the fact, and reconcile yourself to it. If you can't you are unlikely to achieve your goal.

P for purpose

Every action has to have a point. Does this action get me closer to achieving my goal? Why am I doing this? What's the point? Purpose is really important in timelines – those little steps we take along the way to achieving bigger goals. If you don't know why you're doing something you need to ask why you're doing it.

A for aligned

Does the goal fit with the real 'you' – what was described earlier (in Chapter 1) as 'your deepest personal treasure'? Does it connect with the values and the things you want from life? On the journey to goal achievement you will be tested. If you don't feel that what you are doing is an innate part of you then you are so much less likely to be engaged with the actions needed to achieve the goal.

brilliant tip

Everyone thinks they know what's best for us. We're surrounded by people who are willing to advise us - the process usually starts with our parents. Sometimes that advice is great. Often it's not. Often people advise us to do the things that they would like to do for themselves, not what is right for you and the kind of person you are. Check that what you do is aligned with who *you* are, not with whom someone else is.

R for reward

While 'purpose' is about process, 'reward' is about outcome. What do you get from the achievement of the goal (or the time-line) and does the reward mean something for you? The reward can be such a huge motivator. It can be a feeling or a tangible 'something' such as a qualification or a subjective and hopefully accurate assessment that you are 'getting better' as you take the first steps towards managing others. Also, as we said earlier (in Chapter 1) it's perfectly OK if it's 'more cash'. The rewards must be personal to you. Rewards are not universal. Money has never got this writer out of bed in the morning but I know that for some readers it does.

 **brilliant** tip

Think about your goal, shut your eyes and imagine what the reward 'feels' like when you've achieved the goal. Perhaps you are making a presentation to an audience of people eagerly listening to you (in response to having a goal of improving your presentation skills). Perhaps you are making the sale that's been elusive for so long. Maybe you are on the stage at your graduation ceremony collecting a postgraduate certificate in 'X' (fill in the 'X' yourself!) What would that feel like?

C for challenge

If you think back to the first chapter on learning you will recall that the learning process operates in tandem with a degree of struggle. Failure, setback and frustration are common currency here but ultimately good for you if you use them to spur you on.

If you feel that you're being stretched that's great. Say you've just been promoted into a management role and you're trying to develop your knowledge and skills so that you can be a better manager. That process isn't easy. People themselves aren't so easy. We can be difficult, unpredictable, moody, reserved and hard-to-read. But ultimately if you feel that the challenges can be overcome then you will succeed. In fact, without the challenge you are likely to fail – the routine leads to boredom which leads to stasis. The 'stretch' is good.

brilliant tip

Check in with yourself.

'Check in with yourself' means taking an objective look at your behaviour. There are two reasons for doing this:

- to assess how your behaviour impacts other people
- to assess whether or not your behaviour is helping you to achieve your goals.

As we will see later (in Chapter 7), organisations are encouraging collaborative team-based cultures. There's still huge scope for individual achievement of course but personal goals are more likely to be achieved through and with other people. If you have ambition there is a danger that too much self-seeking behaviour can leave others feeling used and manipulated. It can't be overemphasised how important it is to check in with your own behaviour from time to time and to ask what effect your behaviour is having. Collaboration and cooperation are usually the best routes to personal goal achievement. The 'me'-driven focus of career goals should be balanced by the 'we'-focused interpersonal skills that recognise it's with the help of others that we achieve our aspirations.

Take a look back at what we said about 'character strengths' earlier (in Chapter 2). These strengths are the manifestation of our 'values in action'. Those 24 that are listed are all potential strengths. Those that you most closely identify as being authentic to you (if you didn't do the questionnaire) will serve you well in your relations with others. Those who are overly contaminated with ambition lose their real selves (and their strengths and values) and as a result people disconnect from them or only grudgingly help because they have to. Ambition, expressed through career goals, is great. Alienating people is not.

Timelines

A while ago a study undertaken with students found that grade averages increased with short-range planning whereas long-range planning had little effect. In attempting to explain this, the academics concerned indicated that short-range plans can be adapted quickly to change and unpredictability whereas with a big long-range plan adjustments are harder to make. So, for goal-setting this indicates that, while the big goal remains, measuring out small steps along the way gives us the opportunity to:

- measure the effectiveness of the pursuit of the goal – if we can't make the small steps something is going wrong
- make adjustments without jeopardising the big goal
- maintain and even increase performance levels as each timeline is achieved.

With the setting of timelines you can systematically work through the steps to achieving goals if that is the kind of thinker you are. But have no fear if you aren't. Random thinking is initially a good way to start developing timelines. There's an old saying of cartoonist and humourist James Thurber which goes 'Don't get it right, get it written.' It's good advice for the non-linear thinker. Get down all the different steps you think might be necessary, asking, 'If I was going to do this what might the steps be?' Having defined those steps (and asking experts will help) you can then put them in order.

We are at the stage now where the 'head' and heart' tests have been done. Now's the time for your goal to be made real through the development of timelines. We are going to look at two examples of the way in which timelines can be set. The first is a big, potentially life-changing goal – learning a new language for professional development. The second has a shorter-term objective – giving a presentation in one month's time.

The life-changing goal

There are few things which accelerate a career better than being able to speak another language. You become more valuable to an employer that has international operations but it also gives you a far wider range of options should you decided to change jobs. With younger people now changing jobs on average every seven years this is the norm. You also need something to make you stand out. If you have a degree it's something you will share with 40 per cent of the populations in developed countries. That means your degree may not be differentiating enough if it is not directly vocational. Employers will ask, 'OK, what else can you do?'

Below is an example of how timelines can be set for the learning of new language. Note how at each stage there is a clear action to be undertaken that is specific and there is also a definition of success at each of the stages. This example appeared in my previous book *The Luck Habit*.

Let's assume the goal has been taken through the head and heart filters of SMART and SPARC and you have decided that the following goal statement is fit for purpose:

By July 2020 to have passed an A level/baccalaureate in Spanish and be able to converse freely in that language for business purposes.

Your timelines could go like this (I cannot vouch for the accuracy, merely the principle!)

Year one (2015–2016)

Action – To enrol in evening classes at my local college

Achievement – To have mastered basic sentences such as, 'what is your name?' To learn 500 words of vocabulary (10 per week). To know the present tense of key verbs.

Year two (2016–2017)

Action – To continue with evening classes. To visit Spain for two weeks and make a conscious effort to speak only Spanish with Spanish people.

Achievement – A further 500 words of vocabulary. To work through future and past tenses of key verbs.

Year three (2017–2018)

Action – To continue evening classes combined with a monthly visit to a private tutor where I practise my spoken Spanish. Two visits to Spain.

Achievement – To read a Spanish book even if I don't understand all of it (with a dictionary beside me!) To take my first GCSE/national equivalent Spanish exam and pass at the top grade.

Year four (2018–2019)

Action – Fortnightly session with a private tutor. Ten hours per week of study. Two visits to Spain.

Achievement – To pass the A level 'mock' exam beyond minimum grade.

Year five (2019–2020)

Action – As per year four.

Achievement – To pass my A level exam at an A or B grade (or your national equivalent if you are reading this outside the UK).

brilliant tip

Although this example has clear timelines, life doesn't necessarily happen in the way we wish it to. So have your fixed goal, but also think about alternative ways to get there. We can learn something from the way project teams assess risk – they look for the weak points in the timelines and the points where a 'fail' would really jeopardise the whole project. So, do your own bit of risk analysis and have some alternatives if things change.

The short-term goal

A regular theme that runs through Part 2 of this book is the giving of presentations – something that really does seem to give careers a lift if it's done well. In the following example there is a short-term goal – the giving of an important presentation in one month's time – and the steps that might be taken in preparation for its delivery.

Day 1: Define the objective and give myself time to 'play' with possible content in the back of my mind (giving yourself time to think is a very effective way of generating ideas).

Day 7: Put down *all* the ideas I have in connection with the presentation – the audience and its expectations; the content; delivery methods and even likely questions and objections.

Day 10: Develop my structure (around the key points that support the objective).

Day 15: Write my presentation.

Day 20: Prepare my visuals (e.g. PowerPoint or Prezi) and other visual and audio 'props' that may be required.

Day 25: Dry run with a small group working on my body language, my voice and the words I will use.

Day 25: Anticipate likely questions (with the group).

Day 26: Make further adjustments based on the group's feedback.

Day 29: Final practice.

Day 30: Give presentation.

Afterwards: Learning – what can I improve for next time?

How do you 'feel' about the future?

There are plenty of people who don't know, and don't want to know what they will be doing in two, five or ten years' time. This is perfectly natural for them. Many have a sense of what they will be doing in general terms with some happy to go along with the idea that if the future looks interesting or even exciting, then that's enough. This might be you. Goals and timelines will be valuable for specific tasks that need to be completed in the short-term. Other than that don't feel under pressure to swim through the waves when riding with them suits you best.

 **recap**

- Your goal statement should be run through the 'head' and 'heart' filters.

- Use SMART to appeal to the rational side of goal-setting.

- Use SPARC to ensure you are emotionally engaged.

- Check in with yourself to help manage your behaviour when pursuing your goals.

- Big goals should be broken down into stages or 'timelines'.

- Big goals are usually less motivating than the shorter-term pursuit of timelines.

- What sort of person are you? Many people are happy living in the moment with few goals at all.

PART 2

Improving your impact on others

Introduction: Primacy and recency

As this author sits here writing this he is trying to imagine what you, the reader, is like. Are you male or female? Your age? Where are you are locationwise? Where are you in your life? Also, of course I am trying hard to think about why you are reading this book and what you want specifically from it. Perhaps you are thinking about me too? Perhaps you have an image of me in your head. Sometimes when I read a book I hear the words as though the author is reading them and wondering how he (in this case) is saying them. You might even be doing this yourself.

You probably have a stereotype me in your head and I must confess I have a stereotype you. Why don't you write down a few words to describe me now – my age, my hair colour, the car I drive, my domestic circumstances, what I am wearing, what music I like and so on. You can go further if you like – where I am writing this, on what kind of computer, what 'clutter' I have around me, etc. Alternatively, take a look around you now if you are in a public place or do this the next time you are. Select a couple of people at random and write down a few observations about them. What are they wearing – types of clothes (and colours), shoes, glasses? Hairstyles – close cropped, long, expensive haircut? Write down a few words to describe what they might be like as people.

This is something we all do as human beings. It's crazy isn't it – making all of these judgements about people because we want to categorise as quickly as possible. This, however, is important for you in your quest to master effectiveness and impact. In any situation – making a presentation, talking to a prospective client or handling a difficult colleague – people will form an opinion about you very quickly. The point is that once someone has put us into a certain box it's very difficult for that person to take us out of that box and place us in another one in the light of new evidence. Why? Well, the main reason is that once we form an image of someone in our heads, we undergo what's known as 'selective seeing' – looking for evidence that supports the category or box into which we've placed someone and filtering out what doesn't fit with that box.

We do this with our own selves, too, as part of our profound desire for self-understanding. If you have ever done any form of personality profile – from the simplistic ten-question questionnaire on Facebook through to more sophisticated profiling tools such as Myers-Briggs (MBTI) – you have probably absorbed the profile that comes out at the end with great interest. And once we get told a few things about ourselves in the profile (e.g., introvert, sensitive, empathic), typically we (not everyone, but most of us) then look for all the evidence that supports the personality profile, conveniently ignoring much of the evidence which might challenge this.

In one apocryphal though possibly true study 100 people were asked to answer the questions for a well-known personality test and were then given the results. The catch was that every person was given the same results, i.e. the same personality profile. Around 80 per cent said how accurate it was. They can't all have shared broadly similar 'personalities'! So, not only do we do this with other people, we also do this with ourselves.

We like to put people in categories and we might not have many of them. Sometimes we have only three – category 1 people who we like/connect with, category 2 people who we are 'OK' with and category 3 people who we don't like or can't connect with. Most of us are a bit more sophisticated than that, but often not that much more.

Primacy and recency

In a series of studies conducted by Solomon Asch (and since validated by many other studies), it was found that someone's initial impressions of a person's personality traits could influence subsequent interactions, i.e. these initial impressions have a degree of stickability. This won't be a surprise to anyone who believes that first impressions count. In one experiment conducted by Asch participants were given a set of adjectives to describe a person. These were:

Envious Stubborn Critical Impulsive Industrious Intelligent

Another group were given the same adjectives in reverse order:

Intelligent Industrious Impulsive Critical Stubborn Envious

Using a classic five-point rating scale (starting at high and ending with low) one group of people were asked to assess their impression of a person using the first set of adjectives. A second group did the same thing with a person using the second set of adjectives. The second group had a far more favourable impression of the person than the first. Furthermore the first word used, 'Envious' or 'Intelligent', had a disproportionately high impact on the evaluation. This, and other studies, gave great credence to what we call the 'primacy effect' – initial impressions have a great impact on subsequent interactions no matter how accurate or inaccurate they are. This leads to a phenomenon known as 'anchoring'. Anchoring influences processes such as decision-making because we tend to give disproportionate 'weight' to the first information we receive that's helping us to make the best decision, such as a set of statistics or the opinion of a particularly forceful person who likes to get his or her opinion in first. It also means that we tend to make subsequent judgements about people based on the initial 'anchor'.

If you currently aren't good at making a great first impression (though this can be changed as this book will show) there is some good news. What experiments by Asch and others also show is that while we do need to 'anchor' in many aspects of our lives we are not totally fixed in one position by this anchor. The 'recency' effect comes into play too when we take corrective measures in the light of new information. However, the stronger the anchor the harder it may be to absorb new evidence and place the anchor somewhere else.

Psychologists, supported by populist writers such as Malcolm Gladwell (in his book *Blink*) do however also talk of the 'adaptive unconscious' which allows us, in many instances to make quick and *effective* judgements based on little information and lots of instinctive feeling. So, not only do we make quick judgements about others and hold on to them through the need to anchor but these judgements may be somewhat accurate.

So, what does this mean if you are aiming to maximise your effectiveness and impact? It means that when making a presentation you must think clearly about those critical first 30 seconds or so – voice tone, body language and even things such as what you are wearing. It means that when trying to influence a senior manager to take on board your brilliant idea you need to think very carefully about making a powerful argument early on. It means that if you are networking at an industry 'event' (it's coffee break time) you need to think how you introduce yourself, shake hands and make eye contact.

We shall now continue to look at your relations with others. Underpinning this are the effects of 'primacy' and 'recency'.

 **example**

In the 1970s a famous (though in hindsight, terrible!) programme called *The Generation Game* was aired on British TV on Saturday nights. The programme reached its peak towards the end when a single contestant would get through to the final round and he or she could win a large number of different items – mostly things that would be useful around the house. A conveyor belt would pass the eager-eyed and -eared contestant, bearing a series of these household items as a detached voice explained what was going past. It would run for 45 seconds and around 20 items would pass by. The contestant had to remember as many of the items as possible afterwards in a further 45 seconds, being able to take home the items he or she remembered. What occurred, and what many similar game shows display, is that a typical contestant would remember a good number of the earliest items, particularly the first two or three and perhaps also those they particularly wanted. It seems that the primacy effect applies to game shows too.

CHAPTER 5

Communication essentials

'Appearances matter – and remember to smile.'

Nelson Mandela, former president of South Africa

While you cannot *not* communicate, poor communication skills mean little impact which means ineffectiveness. In this chapter we will explore three communication elements that will underpin your effectiveness and impact in different face-to-face situations – language, paralanguage (voice tone) and body language. In Chapter 8 we will look at the written word more closely especially when used in virtual communication systems including social networks and emails.

To close this chapter we look at the listening and questioning skills without which any attempt at mastering the social elements required to be effective at work become irrelevant. This will lead us neatly on to the following chapter which covers a number of aspects of assertiveness including dealing with 'difficult' people and influencing skills.

The three languages

We know how powerful body language is in communication. Those silent signals play an important role in signposting what we are really thinking and feeling and, in particular, the meaning behind what we are saying. Unfortunately, over the years the impact of language, voice tone (or 'paralanguage') and body language including facial movements, have been grossly misinterpreted because people have chosen to misunderstand research conducted by a man called Albert Mehrabian.

You have probably come across the statistics associated with Mehrabian's research. At its worst there are claims that 55 per cent of communication is via body language, 38 per cent from how you say the words you use and 7 per cent from the actual words you use – the fabled 55:38:7 rule. Many people therefore make the ludicrous claim that it doesn't matter what you say as long as you get the body language right based on this research.

What Mehrabian's work does suggest is that where there is a lack of synchronicity – the word 'incongruence' is often used – between body language, voice tone and words, people are likely to take the emotional cues (feelings and meaning) from what the body/face is saying. I think most of us find this believable. However, if I were to come into the room you are in now and shout 'fire' I wonder how much of my body language you would need to see to react? If I shouted, you would get all the feeling and meaning you needed from my voice tone. So, it's also true that these findings may only be true in certain situations, as Mehrabian said. Perhaps typical office environments that aren't in a state of permanent crisis sit here. Let's be clear, words are very important.

What psychologists do generally agree on is that, in most situations, just over 50 per cent of your impact – i.e. getting the message across – in communication comes from the body and facial gestures that are used and just under 50 per cent of your impact comes from the words used and the way you say them (so, broadly in line with Mehrabian's statistics). What Mehrabian really tells us is that if the body language isn't right, we are unlikely to then focus on the spoken message.

In this first section we will look at two situations in which your body language will be central to your effectiveness. These are:

1   in one-to-one situations

2   when speaking more formally in meetings and when making presentations.

brilliant tip

Self-development expert Sarah Litvinoff suggests we 'learn a new body language' – and there is considerable evidence now to show that we can do this even if at first it feels a bit uncomfortable. Start by being aware of how you move and pose. We are constantly being filmed and photographed by phones, hand-held cameras, etc. Your images may live forever in the world of Facebook, Pinterest and Instagram! Take a look at them. How do you come across? Can you make improvements? Take a look at how the confident move around. What do they do physically that makes them more effective in social interactions?

Power posing

'Our bodies change our minds,

and our minds change our behaviour,

and our behaviour can change our outcomes.'

Amy Cuddy, social psychologist

It's very hard to *fake* body language (and impossible with many parts of the face where a number of muscles cannot be moved by conscious thought) but interesting new research is showing that while we have known the effect of body language on others for some time, we are just starting to understand that adapting our own body language in certain situations may also change *us*. Could it be possible that you can affect how you feel about yourself through the adoption of different postures? In a recent study three academics (Carney, Cuddy and Yap, 2010) asked five volunteers to adopt postures related to power. These were 'expansiveness' – how much space your body takes up – and 'openness' – whether your limbs are open or closed. Before asking volunteers to adopt non-expansive/closed and expansive/open postures they carrried out saliva tests to establish levels of testosterone levels (the dominance hormone) and cortisol (the stress hormone). After adopting non-expansive/closed postures, the tests were repeated and it was found that testosterone levels had dropped and cortisol levels had increased. The opposite was the case when volunteers were asked to adopt expansive/open postures – there was an increase in the dominance hormone and a reduction in the stress hormone.

One of the academics involved, Amy Cuddy, is now a strong advocate of what she calls 'power posing'. In power posing you adopt, for one minute, for example, postures that are both expansive and open.

As the final words of the study say:

'By simply changing physical posture, an individual prepares his or her mental and physiological systems to endure difficult and stressful situations, and perhaps to actually improve confidence and performance in situations such as interviewing for jobs, speaking in public, disagreeing with a boss, or taking potentially profitable risks.'

So, for us – those who want to maximise their effectiveness as communicators – it means not only should we adopt positive confidence poses when we, for example, need to give a presentation or have a tough converson but we can also put ourselves neurologically in a good place by literally forcing ourselves to adopt powerful or even dominant poses in private before we need to 'perform'.

▶ brilliant **example**

An example of a 'power posture' can be found below. If you feel powerless in challenging situations power posing can really change how you respond physiologically and this can lead to significant changes in behaviour.

Learning a new language

With such a high degree of importance attached to body language what can you do physically to make an impact and make your workplace interactions more effective? Here are some recommendations that cover the face, then specifically the eyes and then overall body posture and movement.

Face

A woman once approached this author and said that people had told her, when she is about to challenge someone, say something controversial or directly disagree, she smiles a fleeting smile that looks like she's about to kill and enjoy it – it is almost a 'smile of hatred'. She asked me if I agreed. I had been with her for two days and similar thoughts had entered my head. I'd also noticed how her voice tone changed when she disagreed. I didn't answer her question. I asked her what she thought. She said she knew it was a real problem in social interaction and that enough people had told her this for her to believe it to be true. I asked her what was going through her mind at the moment of interjection (e.g. when disagreeing)? She was very honest and said that she rather enjoyed arguing and her competitive nature meant that she got pleasure from 'winning' the argument. It made her feel superior. I said that perhaps the facial expression was a visual signal of what was going on in her head. As our conversation was, of necessity short I asked her what she thought she could do about it now? She wasn't sure but wondered if she would have to, in some way, curb her 'kill to win' instinct.

Because the conversation was so short this was as far we could go (with longer I might have looked at the source of this uber-competitiveness) but it reminded me that it is very difficult to hide the signals of what we are really thinking and feeling because they do leak through our faces. With the body we can quite simply tell our arms to unfold themselves if we sense that the gesture is making us look defensive or arrogant – though we need the self-awareness to recognise what our body is doing and the impact it is having. With the face it's a little different because we can't tell ourselves to stop blushing or to smile genuinely (though we can do a 'fake' smile when we don't get the joke that everyone else understands). Your face will be the visual expression of the performance within it (unless you are an incredible actor) whether that is a sustained performance or a momentary one. Change the internal narrative and then as a rule (though not always) the facial expressions will change too.

The six expressions – and our micro-expressions

Studies by Ekman and Friesen in 1971 in static poses and subsequently supported by Black and Yacoob in 1997 with moving images suggest that six different facial expressions are associated with emotions. These six expressions are:

happiness, sadness, surprise, fear, disgust and anger.

Only one of these – happiness – can be described as positive and smiling will be the visual sign that this is what is being felt. In studies, happiness is always recognised across all cultures. For the other five the recognition levels are also very, very high. So, what does this mean for the communicator, the person who wants to read the facial signals of others? Being accurate in identifying these expressions is one thing but we need to pay particular attention to the leaking of visual cues indicating that someone may be thinking or feeling differently from what is superficially the case.

We leak through micro-expressions – those fleeting manifestations of deeper feelings that we try to conceal – and as effective communicators we need to pay attention to what they really reveal. Later (in the next chapter on assertiveness) we will look at situations in which emotions might be heightened (e.g. when having a difficult conversation). To have impact here you will need to do your best to be aware of the other person's true thoughts and feelings and to adjust your own verbal and non-verbal behaviour accordingly.

brilliant tip

So, given that happiness seems to be the one positive expression and smiling the action associated with it can we learn to smile more? Should we fake it? The answer to faking it is 'no' if it is just not congruent with the other two languages (tone, words) – i.e. you don't actually feel 'happy' – but also, of course, if it's just not right for the situation. However, as you build social confidence and are genuinely happy to be in a situation that five years ago you weren't happy in then the smile will be genuine and congruent with the other languages. Mastery of one skill leads to positive, infectious, non-verbal behaviour.

Eye contact

This cannot be a 'stare-out' of course but eye contact around 50–60 per cent of the time from the speaker is natural. The listener seems to maintain eye contact for slightly longer – probably because he or she is trying to take the meaning from what's being said from non-verbal cues. So, what do you do with your eyes the rest of the time? Studies show that the eyes typically move to a central point just above the other person's eyes, i.e. at the bottom of the forehead, when there is a professional relationship between the two people concerned and to a central point on the bridge of the nose (or perhaps a little further down) when the relationship is more friendly/personal. A more intimate gaze occurs when the eyes go further down, though that clearly would not be appropriate in a 'business professional' setting. We look at what is most interesting to us so make the other person the centre of your visual attention.

What you must avoid is your eyes making sudden movements away from the other person or closing them. Eyes going straight over the other person's shoulder (because someone more interesting has walked into the room) or dropping to the floor because something the other person has said has suddenly made you very uncomfortable and you want to close yourself off, will be read and registered by them.

brilliant tip

One thing that's often done when eye contact needs to be broken is to draw attention to something you can both look at - documents, something of possible mutual interest in the room, coffee or drinks perhaps. These can be good techniques during awkward early exchanges with someone you might not know so well. Of course they might not be needed at all if natural rapport flows right away.

The body language of others

So, making sure your body language is sychronised with what you are saying and how you say it is one thing. Effective communicators know that they also need to read the body language of others to ensure there is rapport. Here are two important points to start.

1 Don't just judge one-off gestures. For example, rubbing under the eye (both men and women do this although women do it less vigorously) can indicate discomfort, deceit or even lying. It can also mean that someone has an itch under their eye. When interpreting body language look for groups or clusters. We consciously and subconsciously read these groups of signals to establish how the other person is thinking and feeling. For example, crossed legs and crossed arms may be accompanied by reduced eye contact and face touching that can paint an overall picture of defensiveness and distractedness, among other things. We then have a choice as to how we respond using the three 'languages' at our own disposal.

2 While we look for congruence we should also look for incongruence. Are voice tone, words and body language out of sync? The face in particular gives away so much due to our relative inability to control it. Shaking the head while saying 'yes' is a good example (though common practice in parts of the Balkans, as mentioned below).

Desmond Morris, a great expert on body language, calls **mirroring** 'postural echo'. With an echo we get a slightly 'quieter' version of the original sound. In body language we mirror the posture of the other person substantially but not exactly. Having done this mirroring and established a comfortable environment for productive communication we can then bring the other person with us through the introduction of other gestures such as hand movements. It's very interesting how often exact

matching will occur in two people who have complete rapport (e.g. both legs crossed, natural eye contact, same arm and hand movements). People can move to this position quite naturally and quickly or with willingness you can **lead** the other person into this very healthy state.

Examples of how you can lead include sitting back in a chair to indicate your own comfort in the situation – but do sit upright – and at times moving forwards to indicate your own eagerness to hear what's being said. Nodding gestures and sincere encouraging words ('Yes, that's interesting') are good too.

Studies of electrical activity in the brain tell us that when two people have rapport the mirroring doesn't just go on visually but also in the brain. Electrical activity seems to be accentuated in similar parts of the brain. It seems that we have neural Wi-Fi systems that tune into each other! We can consciously move towards this healthy position through conscious 'mirroring'. The research by Amy Cuddy and her team that was referred to earlier tells us the body can influence the mind if we adopt certain postures in anticipation of a situation in which we need to be dominant. The same thinking applies in situations in which we need to show other character traits such as empathy. There may be times when we need to hide or **mask** our true feelings because we don't like the other person or we just want to be somewhere else. Perhaps, in the words of Amy Cuddy, we can 'fake it 'til we make it'. We can show the signs of empathy and connection over time if we are willing to adopt the right postures to do this.

Look out too for the **denial** signals in others – those little signals we send when we feel the other person lacks credibility or we don't like him or her. Classic signs include 'eye cut-offs', nose rubbing and shoulder shrugging.

 **tip**

Try to position your body at a small angle to the other person so that you are not directly facing each other, i.e. not too direct, and avoid barriers such as desks whenever you can. Where papers and other documents need to be referred to then across the corner of a desk is fine. If you happen to be a manager (or a budding one) don't do the annual appraisal across a desk – it's amazing how many still do!

Talking to groups

At the end of this chapter we will look at an example of a situation that combines all of the communication essentials featured in the chapter. The situation is making presentations and speeches. Below however, are some key body language tips when speaking to groups. These are just as important when speaking at your team meeting to a group of seven as they are when talking to an audience of 700. These are some key 'dos and don'ts' and some are developed further in the 'Putting it all together' example at the chapter's end.

Move around. Not just on the spot but when speaking for any length of time actually move around. Rigidity suggests nervousness and moving around gets the muscles going and releases the tension.

Don't grip podiums, lecterns or things you have in your hands (slide clickers, etc.).

Keep your **head up.**

Arms out, palms out.

If you are referring to a screen, flipchart, etc. keep your **body open** to the audience.

Try not to look down (at notes or the floor).

Make eye contact with as many people as you can by scanning the room - don't stare excessively at particular audience members.

Vary your 'paralanguage' - tone, pace, etc.

Observe **body language in the audience** as well as being conscious of your own.

Body language and culture

What is clear is that body language and facial gestures are important. What's also clear is that there are variations across cultures although many gestures seem to be shared. For example Bulgarians (and others within the Balkans) will use the head movement most of us typically associate with saying 'yes' for 'no' and vice versa. Although we are told that eye contact is good (and it usually is), in Japan, when conversing with someone more senior, people show respect by looking down – an absolute 'no' in Western cultures. In some Arab states they stand rather closer together when conversing than would be the norm in the West. The story of a Westerner pinned against the wall as he kept walking backwards when conversing with an advancing Arab colleague may be apocryphal but it is believable. When communicating in different cultures it's important to understand the idiosyncrasies (from a Western perspective) that may exist in other cultures.

 **recap**

- Body language and facial gestures play a crucial role in giving the real meaning behind what's being said.

- 'Congruence' or synchronicity across body language, language (the words) and paralanguage (the way you say the words) facilitates understanding of what's being said and the meaning behind it.

- Neuroscience research has shown that not only does our brain change our body but also the most recent research says the body can change the brain.

- 'Power pose' before situations when you need to make an impact.

- Look for 'leakage' – those micro-expressions that are the fleeting signs of what someone really thinks and feels.

- Maintain eye contact but don't 'outstare'. Avoid sudden eye movements away from the other person.

- Clusters of body and facial movements indicate what someone really thinks and feels – not one-off gestures.

- Mirroring/postural echo and matching with your body language help create rapport.

- Keep an open posture – in one-to-one situations and when speaking to a group.

Language and paralanguage

Making an impression using speech

There are so many situations when communicating where your effectiveness will be based on the impression you make. Whether conversing in a one-to-one situation, talking at a meeting or presenting to a group there are some conversational dos and don'ts that will make a big difference to the impression you make.

Consider the other person

We all have different communication styles and although opposites do sometimes attract you need to think about the communication styles of the people you engage with. What is his or her conversational style? While you don't want to 'mirror' slavishly, adopting a style which is in direct contrast to the other person's style can be counterproductive. If you are trying to establish a rapport then creating a synchronous conversation is a good way to start.

> ## brilliant tip
>
> This applies to groups as well as individuals. When making a presentation, the 'in-yer-face' football manager motivating the team at half-time in the changing room style will work in some situations and with some groups. With other groups a more subtle form of exhortation will be needed. Consider carefully what kind of approach will be the most effective.

Maintain objectivity

Not only are many of us prone to generalisation ('that report was terrible') but we are also prone to a lack of specificity, particularly when we state opinions. The impact of your argument, the credibility of your opinion and therefore your effectiveness in certain situations will increase dramatically if you can use specific evidence rather than subjective generalisations to support what you say. Saying 'Sales of product X are 75 per cent down on sales from the previous quarter' is so much more effective than saying 'Sales of product X are hopeless'.

Personal

There is an old saying: the way that someone talks about other people to you will be the way that the same person talks to others about you. Keep gossip out of conversation (or, if you must, save it for the pub) and again, as with the previous paragraph, stick to *relevant* facts.

Don't be the moaner

You know what it feels like to listen to a moaner – the person who endlessly talks about lack of resources, the failings of others, the organisation as a whole and the reasons for them not doing something. In fact, anything but their own failings. It's easy for some of this negativity to rub off on you. This negativity spreads like a virus and you need not only to make yourself immune but also ensure you don't start or spread it. There are very few ways to lose credibility quicker than to be the person that always points the finger of failure elsewhere.

'Trust me'

When someone has to remind you of their source of influence over you it ceases to be a source of influence. My first reaction when someone says 'trust me' is 'Why?' That's my decision – it's not for the other person to advise me to do. Trust is earned on the basis of what we do, not on the basis of what we *say* we are, i.e., trustworthy. Avoid using proclamations about your credibility because the other person will ask themselves why you feel the need to do this. We return to this theme in the next chapter.

The high-rising terminal or 'HRT'

In the past 20 or so years we have seen the rise of what's known as the 'high-rising terminal'. Believed to have originated on the West Coast of the USA or Australia (or both simultaneously) it is expressed as a rising lilt of the voice in the last one or two syllables of a sentence and makes the sentence sound like an apology or, more commonly, an enquiry. The problem with the HRT is that as we detect so much of the meaning from what someone is saying through tone it can be a challenge to discern whether the HRT is a quirk of speech, a sincere enquiry or an apology. Younger readers (younger groups use HRT much more widely) run the risk of not being understood clearly by older generations so use the HRT with contemporaries and avoid it in professional environments.

Making judgements

Many of us make generalisations about people. We might say 'she's extroverted' or 'he's stubborn'. Once we make these judgements (and sometimes we make them in a few seconds) we then go a step further by looking out for the signs that confirm this judgement and ignoring what doesn't. However, those who like to label tend to take another step by creating an opposing characteristic (e.g. extroversion – introspection) and then make a judgement on which they prefer.

 example

Here are some examples of what I see as 'opposites':

rational	intuitive
controlled	emotional
principled	flexible
proactive	pragmatic
honest	secretive
friendly	insular
decisive	cautious
energetic	relaxed

Some of these supposed opposites might not seem to be opposites to you. Our construction of opposites varies from person to person. If you are criticising my constructs here you have fallen into the trap of saying 'I am right and you are wrong', i.e. instant 'judging'. The point is we are both 'right' because we see the world in different ways. This judging mind-set can be a real barrier if you are explicitly (or just in your thoughts) trying to prove that your view of the world is the 'right' one in conversation. It's a very common characteristic. It's also a conversational contaminant.

Mind your language

The Global Language Monitor which scours the internet for new words, declared a few years ago that the one millionth English word had been created. English has many more words than most global languages, in part because it absorbs words and adaptations of words from across the globe. For example, it is widely believed, despite the fact that many English words come from French, that English has three times the number of words that exist in French. This presents opportunities and has given English literature a wonderfully rich base with which to work. However, it also has its challenges because we have so many different ways in which English speakers can express themselves.

With so many words available we have huge scope for ambiguity and passivity. Words can strengthen or weaken the power of your message. Have a look at the words below and then suggest what their effect might be on the person listening.

perhaps, could, possibly, might, maybe, sorry (when repeated)

Sentences such as the following invite negative responses:

'Would you mind…', 'Would it be a problem for you…', 'I am sorry to have to have to ask…', I don't suppose…', Would it be OK if…'

These words and sentences are known as 'softeners'. Using one of them once, in isolation, is fine but in a situation in which you need to assert yourself – asking someone to do some essential work for you by a specific time for example – the repetition of these softening words and sentences weakens your message and invites the other person to misunderstand your needs. You can still be polite and state your needs clearly.

'Dialogue is a form of communication with specific "rules" that distinguish it from other forms. Among the effects of these rules are communication patterns that enable people to speak so that others can and will listen, and to listen so that others can and will speak.'

Barnett Pearce, consultant and coach

'Please stop – I can't get a word in'

A common problem is stopping a person talking who can't or doesn't want to stop. Perhaps the person is boring or meandering from the point. Having a few flattering statements can help:

You made a really interesting point a moment ago and I just want to pick up on it...

Your paralanguage is sincere, enthused, even-paced.

Alternatively, try to repeat the words back in simplified form (and in the style in which they were said):

If I can just summarise, so what you are saying is...

Your paralanguage is clear, to the point, businesslike, but with warmth.

A third technique is to pick on a single word (this comes from the metamodel used by practitioners of neurolinguistic programming) and concentrate on that word to get the conversation back on track:

'I was very worried that we wouldn't be able to meet the deadline...'

'Specifically "worried"?'

'Yes, we were struggling to get the supplier to deliver the packaging...'

Your paralanguage is concerned, empathic, genuinely curious.

 **tip**

Globalisation has meant that a new form of English – jokingly known has 'globeish' – has emerged. It's a more limited form of English but one that allows people from around the world to communicate verbally and understand each other. Globalisation also means that we are likely come into contact with English speakers who aren't from English-speaking countries. By one estimate China will have more people who can speak English than the rest of the first-language English-speaking world by 2025. While that may be an exaggeration many of us who are English speakers will need to speak in a way, professionally, that is understood around the world and quite possibly within our own English-speaking countries. The advice in the 'Mind your language' section above holds true here – avoid ambiguity, passivity and unnecessary 'filler' words. This is just as true for those reading this who aren't from native English-speaking countries. Ask:

'Am I getting the meaning of my message over in the way I want it to be understood?'

The way you say it – paralanguage

Although, theoretically, 'paralanguage' can mean the way we communicate beyond the specific words we use (so it could include facial expressions), it is generally accepted that it refers specifically to the way we say the words we use. The way you say the words you use will depend on the situation you are in. In the next section – 'Putting it all together' – there is an example of how paralanguage can be used when giving a presentation. Other situations will demand different approaches but all situations demand the same considerations. These include:

- **Pitch** – this is usually connected to the importance/ seriousness of the verbal message being sent. A light tone for a less serious message and a heavier, perhaps deeper, tone will create the resonance you seek. Regular, office-based conversation will need a professional, businesslike mid-point.

- **Punch** – keeping to the point in professional environments. Punch can also refer to where you place the emphasis on particular words for effect, such as, 'it's *extremely* important that we remember the sequence for inputting data' with the emphasis on the word extremely.

- **Pace/pause** – slowing down for emphasis and in particular when you are trying to explain something to someone else. Learn to pause when the other person has spoken and while you are speaking – particularly to groups.

- **Passion** – where appropriate give a little feeling but maintain a professional tone. Show you care – especially when speaking to groups.

brilliant recap

- In conversation learn to adapt to the styles of others.
- Avoid generalisations - be specific.
- Avoid remarks about personality - keep to the facts.
- Avoid moaning yourself and keep clear of moaners.
- Use active words and phrases such as 'can' and 'will' rather than passive ones such as 'perhaps' and 'possibly'.
- Ask 'Am I being understood the way I want to be understood?'
- Flattery is a good way to stop someone who has been talking for too long.
- Use the four 'P's in your voice - pitch, punch, pace/pause, passion.

Putting it all together – speaking to groups

The purpose of this section is to put many of the things we have said about the communication fundamentals into practice in a situation in which we can maximise our impact and effectiveness. I've chosen a situation some dislike ('a fate worse than death') but many people have built successful careers solely on – their ability to speak effectively to groups of people. We referred earlier to the synchronicity needed across three core elements in communication with one person or a small number – language, paralanguage and body language. It's no different when we speak to groups.

What is often forgotten is that every kind of presentation – from a few words at a team meeting to a formal presentation to 500 people – has the same fundamental purpose. Speaking to groups is a crucial part of the work we do. Whether you need the group – it could be your team meeting, another team or department, clients or at an industry event – to remember one single thing for the next 20 years or recall a complex financial process or procedure for the next 12 months your ability to present information in a stimulating, structured, memorable way will determine whether you succeed or fail. You do not need to be a great entertainer to be a great speaker. But you do need to utilise core principles, to think with a clear head and put yourself in the audience's shoes.

Get it right and you can speak with real impact. Get it wrong and it can be a real barrier to credibility and career progression. Your effectiveness will be significantly reduced.

Impact and effectiveness – getting your message across

A speaker is a communicator with one central purpose. This central purpose is that the group you are speaking with remember your message or messages for as long as you need them to. This applies whether you are speaking for two minutes or two hours.

You need to bring your content alive for the members of the group so that they remember your message(s). We start with a simple formula to illustrate this:

$$I + E = C$$

That means: *Information (I) + Emotion (E) = Communication (C)*

You need to give *information* – what the group needs to know. You are *communicating* that *information*. The only way people will remember that *information* is if you can touch your audience *emotionally*. Too many speakers think that presentations are only about giving *information*. That if you just say the words, they will be remembered.

So, how do you create this emotional connection? You've probably got a good idea already.

The VHF channel

In the next section on listening we will look at the way in which listening requires the listener to tune in to the message sender and that sometimes it can take a bit of time to pick up the right signal. This applies when speaking to groups. As you speak, you want the listeners – the audience – to tune in to you. To hear what you are saying, take the message you want to send and then remember it. You do this by tuning into the VHF channel of each member of your audience – their **'visual'**, **'hearing'**, and **'feeling'** channels.

V is for visual

You are a fantastic visual aid. In fact you are your number one visual aid when speaking to a group. It's puzzling why so many speakers spend hours preparing PowerPoint slides (often badly), thinking these are their visual aids and totally neglect what they do with their bodies.

Your face

Specifically your eyes. The way you use your eyes will determine whether or not audience members feel you are speaking to them personally. It is so easy to fall into the trap of speaking only to those in the front row or those who are clearly very attentive.

Try to make direct eye contact with at least some members of the audience. Scan the room, making eye contact with people at the extremities of the room (and at the back) so that they feel involved. Some have suggested drawing a 'Z' with your eyes across the room as a way of connecting with the group.

Your body

Your hands and arms are particularly important here. The larger the group the more exaggerated your arm movements need to be – but it must still be natural. A good open posture if you are standing up – try not to be stiff. Think about your legs if you are standing: 15–20 cm apart with your feet pointing at the audience is best. If you are using slides or writing on whiteboards or flip-charts keep an open posture with your body positioned towards the group. Otherwise you will be looking over your shoulder.

Keep the palms of your hands face up and out and your arms moving. This is particularly important if you are sitting down at a meeting and don't have the opportunity/space to physically walk around. Don't fiddle with things – papers, remote controls etc.

Keep your head up (not looking at the floor or at notes) – this makes it easier to keep eye contact (see above).

And finally, notice the body language in the group as well as your own. You get some big clues into what they are thinking and feeling. If they are mirroring much of your own – eager-eyed, open and head movements such as nodding indicating connection – then you know you are getting through.

Other elements

Once you've attended to your face and body you can then look to utilise all those other wonderful 'V' elements available to us.

The room – layout, pictures, posters. Use the whole room. Most speakers and presenters only use the bit around them at the front, for example. Do you even need to begin at the front?

Slides – many people use these as audio aids, i.e. reading the word-congested slide for the audience as though they were unable to read for themselves. It's a 'VISUAL' aid.

Props – physical things that you can show and even share with the group are great.

The Web – youtube.com, vimeo.com, guzer.com, dailymotion.com have wonderful two- to three-minute clips that can add visual and audio impact to your message. Speaking at the next team meeting? Why not kick off with a video clip?

brilliant tip

In many meetings and presentations LCD projectors are used when the speaker wants to use PowerPoint or Prezi. Be conscious of where you are standing – do not bathe yourself in light from the LCD projector. Stand to the side when showing visual aids such as slides or film.

H is for hearing

'Hearing' means the words you use – language – and the way you say them – paralanguage. Let's look at the use of language first. Earlier in this chapter we looked at the use of words and in particular what words to avoid. We know the effect words have on us – particularly if a verbal style becomes persistent (e.g. the overuse of passive words such as possibly, might and maybe). Here are 12 suggestions for the types of words and phrases that will help deliver your message.

1   Use the language of 'we' and not just 'me', as in 'What we are going to do now is...' rather than 'I' as in 'What I am going to show you'. You don't need to do this all of the time but too much 'I' creates a barrier between you and your audience.

2   Avoid 'passive' phraseology. Too much of 'could', 'maybe', 'might' and 'possibly' sends out a signal to your audience that you are not entirely sure yourself of what you are saying or that you don't have an opinion.

3   Be positive. If you believe something, be confident in your opinion: 'If we don't do X then Y will happen'.

4   Use 'bridge' words and phrases to link what you are saying. Phrases such as 'another way of looking at this is...' or 'on the contrary' or a simple 'however'. This helps make your presentation more conversational. A simple 'To move on to my next point' also helps take the audience along with you.

5   Navigate your audience through the presentation: 'As I was saying a few moments ago' or 'To return to my main point'.

6   Give examples to make it realistic. A simple 'Here is an example to illustrate what I mean' or simply 'Let me give an example' or where appropriate 'There is a very recent example of this happening' if people are a little disbelieving.

7   Give your audience an opportunity to challenge their own thinking or to bring in some differing views. Saying 'Another way to look at this is...' or 'One school of thought...' or 'Some people are even suggesting that...'.

8   Inevitably in presentations people will not remember everything you say. But there will be some things you really want the audience to remember. So a phrase such as 'I cannot emphasise this point enough' or 'My key point here is' or even, if appropriate 'If you only remember one

thing from this presentation...'. Do remember that if you do want to emphasise something, slow down and leave a pause afterwards for the audience to digest your point. Even repeat it.

9   Avoid 'basically'. Once is OK but if you start using it regularly people will think that you think they will not understand anything that is more than basic, i.e. they subconsciously think 'The presenter thinks I am stupid'.

10 If you want to make a point that is interesting but not completely linked to your main point tell your audience this is what you are doing: 'I want to side track you for a moment' or 'An interesting aside to this is...' or 'I did hear a story...'.

11 Use acknowledgement points – they help the audience feel more involved. 'I am sure some of you are thinking...', or 'A question I get asked a lot is...'.

12 Signpost the end: 'To summarise' or 'Let's recap the main points' or 'So, to finish, here are the key points'.

brilliant tip

If you are reading from notes use A4-size paper where only the top half is written on. Otherwise your head has to dip to read and your voice drops. Alternatively, use small postcard-sized pieces of card with key words and sentences or a higher table top.

The way you say the words you use – your paralanguage – will be based on the 4 Ps.

● **P – Pitch.** Slow down for effect. A lower tone is also good for effect. A touch quicker (but not too much) to instil energy in the group. Think about your head position as this affects tone. A dipped head means a voice that is likely to 'dip' too which might start to bore the audience. The pitch of your voice should reflect the nature of the presentation you are giving (e.g. serious, light-hearted, grave, etc.) although incongruent 'tricks' such as black humour can also work.

- **P – Punch.** Punch means keeping to the point. Keep sentences short and clear and use language that the group will understand. Don't use words that might show off your language skills but might be above the level of the audience. This is really important if you are presenting in a language which is not the native tongue of some group members – increasingly likely in this globalised age. This isn't about dominance. It is about control. It is about confidence (but not superiority).

- **P – Pause.** Give the group time to absorb what you have said. Use pauses for effect and for impact – when you have a particular point that you want to resonate with the group. Remember that what seems like a long time to you is a welcome break – a chance to think – for the audience. Pauses are the punctuation marks of your presentation.

- **P – Passion.** Above all if you don't 'feel' it no one else will. Emphasise those emotive words with feeling. Also use your body for more emphasis.

Dialogue with the group

Once you have finished speaking you may then enter into a dialogue with the group. In a meeting this may have a more relaxed feel – although not always. In a formal presentation the atmosphere may be slightly different – in part depending on the numbers of people watching. Your dialogue will typically take the form of questions and answers. There are two types of questions. Those you ask for and those that come unsolicited.

Questioning techniques

- Ask questions directly – 'Does anyone have any questions?' – is a common method though not perhaps the best as the language is very passive. Try to be more confident/ assertive in your language with your tone clearly making the assumption that people *will* have questions. For example, 'I know this is something that some of you feel very strongly about so I would be pleased to answer your questions.' Then there is the assumptive 'What questions do you have?'

- Listen to the whole question. Sometimes your relief that you have a question you can answer (particularly if you are nervous about this) makes you prone to 'premature articulation'. Refer to the advice on this in the 'Listening' section of this chapter.

- Thank the questioner – 'That's a great question' or 'I am really glad you asked me that question' or 'It's great that you've picked up on one of my key points'. But do this for all though – if you don't praise/acknowledge the validity of my question I might wonder why, when you have with others.

- Just as you would in a one-to-one conversation, good practice is to repeat the question back. This does three things.

   - It ensures you have understood the question and also, if necessary, you can clarify.

   - If you are talking to a larger group repeating the question means that everyone hears it (sometimes the questioner may have his or her back to parts of the audience).

   - It gives you thinking time.

- If you need more time (and even if you don't) a good technique is to throw the question back to the audience – 'Have any of you found yourself in a similar situation? How did you find yourself dealing with it?' You may find yourself not even having to answer the question yourself.

- Have pens and paper handy for everyone so they can write their questions down during your presentation is an alternative method – this helps overcome the awkward silence if no one has a question.

- And when you have answered it check that you have answered the question to the person's satisfaction.

When you're not getting much back from the group

- Ask a question yourself that you know the audience will have an answer to or a strong opinion about (prepare one or two in advance).

- Brief someone you know in the audience to have a question ready to ask you (only) if you anticipate a reluctance to ask one.

- Have a preprepared question that you can ask yourself – but don't be too quick in asking it. 'A question I get asked a lot is...'.

- If you genuinely want questions then a final solution is the battle of wills option – hang on in there until someone does ask one.

You get a question/statement you can't answer/respond to...

- If you don't know the answer then say so and promise to get back to the person with an answer.

- As above, seek out possible answers from other members of the audience. If you know there are experts in the audience you can seek their help.

- Sometimes you get people who strongly disagree with you. Don't rise to any bait but keep control: 'I appreciate this is a sensitive issue and there are different opinions about it. I can only offer my own opinion.'

▶ brilliant example

At a public inquiry into the press and its behaviour (the Leveson Inquiry), held in the UK in 2011–2012, global media mogul Rupert Murdoch used a very interesting technique for defusing a situation in which he was clearly very uncomfortable. This is only recommended if you are in a tough situation with a very 'difficult' questioner. What Rupert Murdoch did was to finish answering the question, pause and then interrupt the reply, putting the questioner off his rhythm: 'I am just reflecting back on your last question and another thought has to come to mind....' It certainly isn't a technique I recommend you use too much but might help in very specific circumstances.

F is for feeling

If you want your audience to remember something, or go off and do something or to think in a certain way you are going to need them to 'feel' something. The feeling will give them the motivation to deliver the action you require. The 'V' and 'H' of 'VHF' support this but what you say does too. Here are some suggestions.

- **The past** – 'Do you remember what it felt like when…?'
- **Stories** – 'There once was a wise old hermit….'
- **Impending disaster** – 'If we don't do xxx, the future could look like yyy….'
- **The future** – 'Imagine what it will feel like if….'

↻ brilliant recap

- Speaking effectively to groups is a brilliant career accelerator.
- The main purpose of any talk, speech or formal presentation to a group of people is that the group remembers your key message(s).

- Remember that a speaker is a communicator who understands that emotional connection means information retention: $I + E = C$.

- Use the VHF – visual, hearing and feeling – channels to create that emotional connection.

- You are your number one visual aid.

- Use assertive language that delivers your message in the way you want.

- Use tone, pause and passion for impact and to vary the way the message is delivered.

- Stories and anecdotes engage the group.

Listening and questioning

You often hear of somebody talking too much. Nobody could be accused of listening too much.

James Borg, author of *Persuasion*

A few years ago this author sat on a panel of expert trainers. There were four of us. We were being asked lots of questions by an audience of human resources trainees. At one point we were all asked a great question: 'If you could only run training courses on one soft skills subject what would it be?' Three out of the four of us said listening (the other incidentally said 'feedback' – also covered in this book). So, why did we choose listening? The reason, at least for me, is that there is no area of human inter-action excellent listening skills are not integral to. With great listening skills comes the need for insightful questioning, of the kind that can only occur when you have truly tuned in to what the other person is saying.

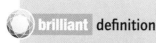 **definition**

In his classic book *Microserfs* Canadian writer Douglas Coupland invented a new word – 'interiority'. He described it as 'being inside someone's head'. It's a very good description of what a great listener does. It implies strongly that empathy is central to effective listening, which it is. A great definition of **empathy** is 'I feel with you' though this must not be confused with sympathy ('I feel for you').

Listening is a life skill

Great listening is a life skill – think about how so many people blame the breakdown of their relationships on 'lack of communication'. But at work, too, it's central to some of those key elements of personal effectiveness such as assertiveness, influencing, negotiation and networking. Think also about your meetings. Sometimes they feel as though they are arenas in which a lot of talking goes on but not a lot of listening. Implicit is a feeling that many participants think 'my opinion is better/ more valid than yours'.

Author Zig Ziglar talks of the radio station we have in our heads – WII FM. This stands for 'What's In It For Me?' If you want to influence, persuade, negotiate or assert yourself (for what we call a 'win-win' solution') the other person will immediately ask the WII FM question. You can't answer that question if you don't understand the needs, wants and interests of the other person. The other person is thinking, 'OK, you want me to do this, what's in it for me?' and you can address this internal driver by saying, 'You've said this is particularly important to you, so I suggest…'. But you can't do this if you haven't asked questions and listened.

Listening barriers

Most of us prefer talking to listening so we immediately have a primary, perhaps even primal, barrier to being a good listener. Author of *Persuasion* James Borg says that we think much faster than we talk (up to four times faster) so there is much space for distraction as the other person talks. However there are several other reasons why we either have a compulsion to speak (and thereby not listen) or to disengage partially or completely. They might include:

- 'I disagree with what the other person says' (in which case you are preparing your counter argument or actively voicing your disagreement)
- having a 'busy' mind – you're thinking about other things
- lack of rapport between us
- 'I'm very busy – I don't have time for this'
- he or she is boring
- 'I'm tired'
- other priorities (perhaps the conversation is a priority for the other person but not for you)
- stress
- 'I've got something even more interesting to say' (in which case you are either saying it or preparing what you are going to say)
- the other person isn't particularly credible to you (this is surprisingly common – think of the people you work with who aren't credible to you and how your conversations runs along with those people)
- 'I want to "win"' – the competitive streak kicks in so that all we want to do is force our views on the other person

The consequences of any of these are that you mentally withdraw from the conversation. You are still physically present of course but you are now either:

- preparing your response – in which case you've stopped listening because you can't be listening and preparing your response at the same time, or

- thinking about something else (the next meeting, what you're doing tonight, etc.).

Creative, committed listening

Educationist Mark Brown (referenced several times in this book) talks amusingly about 'premature articulation'. It's where people can't resist the temptation to talk rather than continue to listen. It's often the consequence of the 'head chatter' that goes on in your head as you latch on to the first thing you agree or disagree with. The head chatter occurs for the many reasons listed in the 'Listening barriers' section above. Mark Brown refers to this as 'critical listening' – effectively listening to criticise and therefore formulate premature responses. The greater the level and depth of conversation in your own mind the less you are able to listen properly to what's being said – and truly understand why it's being said.

If critical listening sits at one end of the scale then what Mark Brown calls 'creative listening' sits at the other (see the diagram below). Creative listening means that you don't just keep quiet when someone speaks but that you, in the words of Douglas Coupland, live 'inside someone's head'.

Mark Brown's critical/creative scale

| 0 | 5 | 10 |
| CRITICAL | | CREATIVE |

 **exercise**

Take a look at the scale above. Although this is a subjective exercise its purpose is to help you think about your own listening style. Having had a look at the barriers listed above (and assessed how many of these apply to you) now try to plot where you sit on the scale between 1 and 10. Once this is done, ask what you can do to push yourself a couple of points further up the scale. Look at the 'Committed to listening' section and apply some of the suggestions in your own life. The aim here is not to be a 10 (though that will be important if you are a social worker or therapist) but to start pushing in the right direction. It's amazing how often we remember people who we feel really listen to us. You will make a lasting impact if you do this.

Committed to listening

You can actively stop yourself getting lost in your thoughts. As we have seen in this chapter there are things we can do with our body, voice tone and words that show the other person our commitment to listening and in some cases these will force us to listen. These include the following.

- Not seeing conversation as a 'competition' – it's all too easy to improve someone else's story with one of our own, thus turning the conversation into a verbal sparring session.

- Challenge your own disagreement with questions that do not reveal your disagreement: 'That's an interesting perspective, why do you see it that way?' or 'What's your experience of this? I am interested to hear how…'.

- Use a calm tone to signal encouragement. Nodding your head tells the other person you are actually listening.

- Your body sends out many 'silent signals'. Use a positive, open posture, including having the palms of your hands open to signal overall openness. Neuroscience has discovered much about the effects of body language on not just the other person but also ourselves – see the example of 'power posing' earlier in this chapter.

- Be comfortable with silence in conversation. This serves two purposes.

  - The other person often moves into the silence by continuing to speak (a lot of coaches do this).

  - It gives you thinking time. You can even say something like 'I am just thinking about what you said' to give yourself time and send a signal that you have been listening.

- If you're very tired and finding it hard to focus why not just agree to meet at a better time to have the conversion. You don't need to reveal your tiredness: 'I would like to give this conversation the time it deserves. Why don't we meet…'.

- Play back and interpret what you have heard – but only when you have the full story.

- A lot of people are prisoners of their own view of the world. They see their world as the only world. Understanding that ours is just one world among seven billion releases a mental brake that stops us from trying to be the centre of everyone else's universe as well as our own.

- Not only are some people prisoners of their worldview but they may also be 'prisoners of prejudice'. Prejudice, which means to prejudge, will immediately create a bias in your thoughts. Begin all interactions with an open mind.

brilliant tip

A good trick for disciplining yourself to listen is to actively seek to confirm what you have heard. You clearly can't repeat what you think you have heard if you don't listen. So, saying, 'So, what you are saying is...' or 'I just want to confirm what you said you wanted...' is a good way to check understanding but it also keeps your mind focused on what's being said rather than being lost in your thoughts.

brilliant recap

- Consider all the situations in which listening is important in your working life.
- Be aware of your own barriers to listening.
- Be a good, trusted person to talk to.
- Actively move yourself up the 'creative listening scale'.
- Use the right language – verbal and non-verbal.
- Actively show attentiveness and accuracy through paraphrasing and empathy.
- Your world is not the only world. Be prepared to step into another's world, i.e. show true empathy.
- Use insightful questions to move the conversation forward (see below).

Questioning

'To be able to ask a question clearly is two-thirds of the way to getting it answered.'

John Ruskin, social thinker and philanthropist

Remember the old radios when you had to turn a dial to tune in to a particular station? We called them 'wireless' radios. One of the problems with a wireless radio was that you had to keep adjusting the tuning dial to exactly the right spot so that you could get the channel you wanted and hear it with clarity. It took a bit of time but eventually you got there. Sometimes the station tuned out again a little and you had to fiddle with the dial to get it back again.

Listening and questioning is often like this. Tuning in with open questions and then when you are getting closer (understanding what the other thinks, feels, believes) asking more probing questions to get the right point. And sometimes you need to retune if you find that you aren't on the same wavelength.

Implicit with listening is the facility to ask the right, insightful questions. This insightfulness comes hand-in-hand with great listening. Imagine a scenario in which a colleague has asked you for some figures when you are busy. How do you respond? Do you provide a hesitant, passive response such as, 'I'm sorry, I'm sort of busy at the moment. Is it OK if I get them a bit later?' Do you instead actually ask the right questions to maximise the effectiveness of the interaction? There are two questions you need to ask here in what is a classic time management situation. The first, 'What specifically do you need from me?', or to confirm that you have understood what has been asked for, 'You're looking for the figures for sales projections for each product for the next quarter – is that right?' And then, again specifically the second question, 'When do you need them by?'

Here's where we can now use what's called the questioning 'funnel'.

▶ brilliant example

The funnel starts with an open question, i.e. the open end of the funnel. So, in the time management scenario we are looking at, 'What specifically do you need from me?' and 'When do you need the figures by?' are good examples of this. The second step is a probing question, i.e. where the funnel starts getting narrower. These are 'open' to get more information and they usually start with 'who, what, why, where, when, how'. An example: 'How are you going to be using the figures as I want to make sure they are presented in the right way?'

We then finish with a closed question to confirm what's been understood or agreed. In the example above: 'You're looking for the figures for sales projections for each product for the next quarter – is that right?' is an assumptive closed question in that it makes an assumption (based on excellent listening!) which the other person can then confirm or put right. There may be a number of 'funnels' within a conversation.

brilliant tip

Question types to avoid are those prejudicial questions that imply an opinion or bias in the questioner. Examples include, 'Do you want this before lunch or for the 2 o'clock meeting as usual?' or 'Why are you doing it that way?' The second example hints that the questioner doesn't agree with it being done *that way*.

Great questions

Here are some further examples of good question types that will maximise your effectiveness in one-to-one interactions.

- A simple 'Now tell me…' or 'What do you think about this? or 'How's this looking from your perspective?' are good starts because they invite the responder to contribute and you get to understand what the other person is thinking.

- **Probe** – where you want to dig more deeply and for where the original open question hasn't provided enough information. 'I'm interested in knowing a bit more about this, what specifically is it that you enjoy about...?' or a simple 'Tell me a little more about how you feel', are good examples.

- **Clarify** – Establishes parameters for clarity: 'So, I just want to be clear, are we talking only about...' or 'So, what you're saying is...'.
- **Summarise** – 'I just want to be sure I've understood...' or 'So, to summarise, the problem is x and you're suggestion is that we do y to solve it'.
- **Conclude** (if necessary) – 'So, we've agreed...'.

brilliant impact

Remember to make use of the other person's name – particularly true if you don't know the other person well. This shouldn't be overdone but most of us love to hear the sound of our names. It emphasises personal connection.

Although there is some formality implied here these specific question types fit comfortably into the natural flow of conversation. In situations where you need to maximise your own effectiveness and impact it is essential that you can work your way into other people's thoughts and feelings so you build stronger relationships with people. After all you can only get results by working through and with people. Some people seem to act as though they get results *despite* people.

brilliant recap

- Brilliant questions lead to brilliant insights.
- Use open questions for information and understanding.
- Use the question funnel to achieve clarity.

- See questioning as a way of tuning in to another person's thoughts and feelings.
- Good questions are essential for the core areas of effectiveness such as assertiveness and time management.

CHAPTER 6

Assertiveness and influencing

'... simultaneously holding my own ground while being profoundly connected to the other person.'

Barnett Pearce, consultant and coach

This chapter is split into two main sections:

- assertiveness, and
- influencing.

Then we put it all together at the end.

Assertiveness

Being assertive makes so many of the interactions you have with others more productive. It is essential when you are reaching agreement, influencing, receiving feedback, having a 'difficult' conversation and even speaking at meetings. We have covered some of these topics (e.g. receiving feedback) already.

In this chapter we are going to take the essential communication skills already covered (in the last chapter) and apply them to situations in which your needs and interests must be met but where good relations with others, including work colleagues, are maintained. Our guiding philosophy is 'win-win' and this is explained in more detail in the next section. Barnett Pearce's quote at the beginning of this chapter very neatly gets to the heart of true 'win-win'.

After looking at our guiding 'win-win' philosophy we then look at the core principles of assertiveness and work through an example of their application. In the second part of this chapter we then concentrate on one aspect of assertiveness – influencing – looking at different strategies and working through two examples.

The most important element in assertiveness is what you do in preparation for the situation in which assertiveness is needed. We call this the 'mental rehearsal'. This topic is covered in both parts of this chapter.

The advantages of assertiveness

So, what advantages does assertiveness bring? Why is it so important to personal effectiveness? Here are several of the reasons.

- Assertive behaviour means you state clearly your needs, wants, interests, ideas and opinions. This increases the chances that people will listen to you and that your needs in particular will be met through the use of skills such as influencing, negotiation and persuasion, all of which have their roots in assertiveness.

- However, assertive behaviour is not just about you and what *you* want. At its heart is the maintenance of effective relationships with colleagues.

- Assertiveness increases effectiveness. Effectiveness gains credibility. Credibility gives greater influence.

- As you see results from your assertive approach you build confidence in your dealings and relationships with others.

- Confidence in yourself means being less threatened by others – you see their strengths.

- Assertiveness means you take responsibility for your behaviour which gives you more control over it.

● It takes a lot of energy out of you if you have to worry about difficult interactions with others. If you have an internal system for this it becomes easier.

The three behaviours: assertiveness

Assertiveness is one of three possible behaviours used in getting (or not getting) what we want – aggressive and passive/non-assertive behaviour are the other two. Below is a definition of assertiveness. After this we look briefly at aggressive and passive behaviour, defining them and giving examples of how they manifest themselves before concentrating on developing an assertive approach.

 **definition**

Assertiveness is:

● saying what you want, think, need, feel or believe

● saying it honestly, directly, *appropriately*

● respecting the rights of those we are addressing.

This definition is based on the work of assertiveness experts Kate and Ken Back whose expertise features here alongside that of Manuel Smith – author of *When I Say No, I Feel Guilty.*

Recognising passivity, recognising aggression

The emphasis in this book is on assertive behaviour and its application in many different situations. However, you also need to recognise the signs of aggressive and passive behaviour both from within yourself and in other people.

Passive/non-assertive behaviour

 **brilliant** definition

Passive behaviour involves expressing ourselves in a way that lacks clarity about what we want, and leaves us open to manipulation or to being misunderstood.

These are some of the signs that demonstrate passive behaviour.

Body language

- Lack of eye-to-eye contact (e.g. looking down or actively away from the other person).
- Defensive body language (e.g. 'closed' posture, hands covering parts of the face, shrugging).
- Fidgeting with your hands.
- Reactive body posture (e.g. backing away).

Language

- Apologising too much (e.g. 'I'm so sorry, I really am... really am sorry').
- Not prioritising your needs (e.g. 'I am a bit nervous of my boss, not that this is important').
- Saying 'yes' all the time (e.g. when being asked to do things at work when in the middle of something else).
- Agreeing without questioning.
- Regular use of 'filler' words such as 'perhaps' and 'maybe'.
- Putting yourself down with vague generalisations (e.g. 'I am no good with figures and I never will be').
- Regularly seeking permission (e.g. 'Is it OK if...?').

Paralanguage

- Inconsistent speech patterns (e.g. pausing, speeding up/ slowing down).
- Subdued or weak tone.
- Sentences that tail off.
- 'Shaking' in the voice
- A strain in the voice.

Aggressive behaviour

 **definition**

Aggressive behaviour occurs when we force our views on others and/or deny rights to others that we believe we have ourselves. Here are some of the classic signs of aggressive behaviour in action.

Body language

- Lots of facial activity (e.g. glaring, raised eyebrows, outstaring, facial 'thrusting' especially the chin, head shaking).
- Invading the other person's personal space.
- Exaggerated body movements (e.g. fingers pointing, fists pumping, crossing and uncrossing arms indicating impatience and lack of approachability).

Language

- Interruption (e.g. 'It's all very well you saying that, but...').
- Manipulation (e.g. 'I know we can rely on you. It's you we come to when things get difficult').
- Unwanted 'advice' (e.g. 'If you want my advice you should...').

- Blame (e.g. 'We'd be all right if the marketing department knew what it was doing').
- Challenging (e.g. 'So, what makes you think this will work then?')
- Personal non-specific criticism (e.g. 'You're just not tough enough for this kind of work').
- Exaggerated stubbornness – even when an idea is in your interests.

Paralanguage

- Firm/fluent…sometimes fast.
- Sarcasm.
- Raised voice.
- Accusatory tone.
- Interrupts.
- Tone indicates opinion is fact which makes it hard to disagree.

(The positive, effective use of the 'three languages' that facilitate an assertive approach were covered in Chapter 5 'Communication essentials'.)

How to be assertive

There are five elements to assertiveness.

1   Decide what you want, think, need, feel or believe.

2   Run through your 'mental rehearsal'.

3   Use the three languages.

4   Avoid manipulation.

5   Aim for 'win-win'.

We will look at each of these elements in turn.

1. Decide what you want, etc.

These should be absolutely specific, for example:

- 'A colleague (of equal status) who I rely on to provide me with monthly figures has been providing me with poor-quality work over the last three months. I need him to understand how the figures have to be presented to me each month so that they can be incorporated into my report for senior management.'

- 'I believe the proposed changes to our team structure will not be beneficial to the work of the team and I need to express this view at the next team meeting. It's a situation in which I hold a minority view.'

- 'I want to have a confident voice and positive body language at my promotion interview.'

2. Run through your mental rehearsal

There are three acknowledged behaviours – passive, aggressive and assertive. As we have seen with passive behaviour we fail to state what we want or do so in such a way that our wants and needs are likely to be misinterpreted. In aggressive behaviour we fail to acknowledge the needs and rights of others. Neither of these is productive behaviour if you want to preserve strong relationships. Sometimes aggressive behaviour manifests itself because the aggressor doesn't care about the needs and rights of others. Often it comes out because of the nature of the mental rehearsal that plays out in our minds prior to an interaction requiring assertiveness.

The mental rehearsal has two elements. The first is that we visualise the situation in which we are likely to find ourselves. Making a difficult presentation at the next meeting? It helps to 'actualise' your presence in the meeting ahead of it. The second is the inner conversation you have with yourself about the impending situation and the tone this 'inner conversation' takes.

We call this the 'inner dialogue' and differentiate, as the Backs describe it, between a 'sound inner dialogue' and a 'faulty inner dialogue'. The faulty inner dialogue will either lead to passivity or aggression depending on the nature of the inner conversation. The sound inner dialogue gives the best chance of a productive dialogue with another person or between you and a group. So much for the theory – how does this play out in the real world? Here is an example.

▶ brilliant example

Situation: *You want to give feedback to a colleague (Pat) who is making a lot of mistakes and they are affecting your own ability to do the job properly. She takes criticism badly.*

Example of faulty inner dialogue: 'If I mention these mistakes to Pat she's going to respond badly. That won't be good news. It's going to be a struggle but if I need to stand up to her and have an argument I will. She needs to know what I think.'

There are several problems with this. The first is, that while it is good to consider possible responses and prepare yourself for them, this one is predictive – Pat will 'respond badly'. It then becomes aggressive in intent – 'If I need to stand up to her and have an argument I will'. This inner dialogue is setting up potential conflict. 'She needs to know what I think' doesn't allow for you needing to know what Pat thinks. It's all one way.

Example of sound inner dialogue: 'I need to make sure these mistakes don't happen again because they are affecting my ability to get the job done but I do need to keep an open mind about this. There may be factors I am unaware of. I will state the facts clearly and give Pat the chance to respond. It might be a difficult conversation, because Pat is sensitive but if I stick to the facts, remain calm and in control of my own thoughts and feelings then I give us the best chance of a productive outcome.'

You start by stating your goal – 'to make sure these mistakes don't happen again' – but you don't predict the cause of the problem. You have a clear grasp of the facts and allow space for Pat to present her side. You acknowledge that it might be difficult but you identify the behaviours needed to get the best result.

3. Use the three languages

The definition of assertiveness includes the word 'appropriately'. There are many ways to express what you want and one false reading of assertiveness says that it is about you and the issue of your needs. It's not quite like that. The definition also refers to 'rights'. So if we link 'appropriate' approaches and 'rights' together one might say 'I have the "right" to be listened to'. And you do. But so does the other person. So an appropriate approach is to recognise your 'right' while adopting appropriate use of the three languages (see the last chapter), which means acknowledging that this is a dialogue between equals who both or all have rights and needs to be met. A good rule is to say that whatever rights I think I have – e.g. to be listened to; to be treated fairly; to have an opinion – I must also give to the other person or group. Rights work both ways.

4. Avoid manipulation

Manipulation occurs when someone gets you to behave according to his or her rules, opinions and values. When you live by your rules and judgements then you immediately set up a barrier against manipulation. To be effective here requires self-awareness – what are your values?

Your professional effectiveness can be driven by a series of affirming statements that provide the motivation and pro-pulsion in the different situations in which your assertive approach is needed. These affirming statements also provide a defence mechanism against manipulation. They remind you of your self-worth, build confidence and facilitate effectiveness. Where confidence is low, assertive approaches become harder to visualise and enact with the consequence being that others may manipulate you. This manipulation may not even be intentional. These affirming statements can be stated as a form of self-talk and they can even become personal mantras that remind you of your self-worth and rights. They must be seen as governing principles, not as worthy statements to be admired rather than enacted. Examples can include the following but you should look to develop your own (and some might be job-specific):

- I have the right to be treated with respect and I will respond when I feel I am not.
- I will defend my needs and interests but I do understand that others have the right to do this as well.
- I have the right to have opinions and for those opinions to be heard, as do others.
- I have fresh ideas and the right to express them.
- I have the right to say 'no'.

5. Aim for 'win-win'

'Win-win is a frame of mind that constantly seeks mutual benefit in all human interactions. Win-win means that agreements or solutions are mutually beneficial and satisfying.'

Steven Covey, author

In the third element we drew attention to the communication skills needed in assertiveness. In aiming for 'win-win' we see those communication skills being used to maximum effect.

Thinking through 'win-win'

Win-win is the desirable outcome in most situations. One interpretation of win-win is that you get what you want (you achieve your goal) and so does your colleague. However, there is also a second 'win'. The second win is the preservation of the relationship. You can get what you want through aggressive behaviour but, in most situations, particularly when you work with the person concerned, you want to be sure that your good working relationship continues. Aggressive or manipulative behaviour can leave feelings of anger, resentment and frustration. However, there are times when true 'win-win' isn't possible or occasionally even desirable.

The diagram below applies to assertiveness in everyday workplace situations – it has been significantly adapted from a classic model for resolving disagreement and conflict by Kenneth Thomas and Ralph Kilmann. As you will see, it identifies four situations: 'win-win', 'lose-lose', 'win-lose' and 'lose-win'. These refer specifically to you and your needs. As we have already established, in any situation in which you need to assert yourself with another person – perhaps someone hasn't been supporting you in the way you need or a colleague has made a request that is difficult for you to meet because you are busy – you need to be clear on your needs.

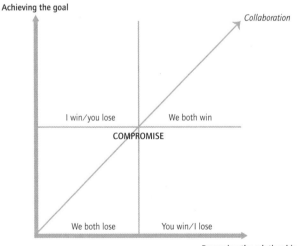

The four boxes

This section includes a description of these four outcomes, why they happen and circumstances in which each might be desirable (even 'lose-lose').

- **Win-win:** Aiming for win-win means that not only are you clear on your own needs but you are also clear on the other person's needs as well. It means that both parties get what they want but that the relationship is preserved, perhaps even strengthened, by the collaborative nature of the search for a solution and by the fact that the outcome has been positive as well. Neuroscientists have even shown that rapport, connection and relationship efficacy (getting a result) trigger the release of pleasure-inducing chemicals within the brain. Because we like what makes us feel good we want more of it.

  Collaboration takes time and often requires creativity in the search for an optimal solution. It also requires both parties to want to seek something better than compromise, which is when we both get a degree of what we want – 'the essential need(s)' – but not everything. In compromise a relationship status quo is preserved.

- **I win, you lose:** So, why might this happen? In certain situations requiring assertiveness, such as a financial negotiation when you are trying to obtain the best price for a car you are buying, your concern is to get the best price possible. You still need to respect the rights of the other person as a fellow member of the human race but your concern is your need. The seller can look after his or her own. This kind of situation rarely occurs in the workplace or at least it shouldn't do so. However, if the person is uninterested in your needs (even though you are initially interested in his or hers) – often expressed through aggressive behaviour – then you may decide to walk away or to 'look after yourself'.

It must be emphasised that the likely consequence of an 'I win, you lose' approach will be relationship damage. Fine if you are never going to see the person again; not so good if you are.

● **I lose, you win:** Is there something that's not so important to you but it is to the other person? It's late in the day, your colleague is under pressure, you less so, he or she asks for help. It's not so convenient for you because you've got an opportunity to get home on time for once, but you know your relationship with this colleague is important so you help out. This is a mutually supportive relationship. There will be times when you need the help of your colleague. You want to make a good impression.

● **We both lose:** So why would you both want to lose? Sometimes, having a battle just isn't worth it. You both lose and you see the uglier side of each other. Besides, what you want doesn't mean that much to you. Pick your battles.

Here is an example of when assertiveness skills can be used productively. Imagine you are the person who has this challenge. How would you deal with it? Read the text below and think for a few moments before reading on.

▶ brilliant example

Problem: *'I need to have a difficult conversation. I have a situation in which a colleague talks about me behind my back to my boss and to colleagues. Frankly, I think using gossip and misinterpretation of my actions are being used to cover my colleague's inadequacy. It's easier to blame me.'*

This is a situation you have to think clearly about what you want the outcome to be (your goal) – e.g. I need this gossip to stop.

▶

You need to prepare your assertive inner dialogue. It might go along the lines of:

'I will approach John with an open mind but with my evidence to hand. I will give him every chance to speak and present his point of view which is his right. He may be embarrassed and/or emotional or he may get angry but I can handle it. I will keep calm, in control, keeping to the objective facts at all times. I will remember that my goal is to stop the comments about me, not to "win".'

What is key here is that you have some *specific* examples of when this behaviour was displayed and so the need for preparation cannot be overemphasised. Specific, objective examples prevent denial. If it's vague, it's easy to deny. You may believe that this is because the colleague is hiding inadequacy but evidence for this may be hard to find, so don't bring it up. It's up to the person to look into the reasons for it – your goal is for it to stop.

You must keep control of yourself and your emotions throughout – clear language, calm but professional paralanguage – as it is possible that the other person will react emotionally (anything from tears to anger) and adopt an open body posture. If you have to deal with emotional behaviour, keep quiet and let the other person finish. Deep breaths if necessary. If you know the person well you may have an idea as to how he or she will react. Remember too that expressions of emotion can be used as a manipulative tool by some to make us feel sorry for them (e.g. anger to provoke 'fear', tears to provoke 'sympathy').

You may need to express your own feelings. A classic way to state this is just to say, 'When you do/say xxxx it makes me feel like yyyy. I am sure that is not your intention but that is how I feel.'

Earlier (in Chapter 4) we looked at two types of goals – problem-solving goals and opportunity goals. Here we have looked at a problem goal. The influencing section of this chapter looks at an opportunity goal – presenting new ideas at a meeting (where there may be challenges).

 **recap**

- Assertive behaviour allows you to express your needs, meet them and preserve relationships. It is an essential skill for professional impact and effectiveness.

- Aggressive behaviour denies rights, uses force and manipulation and ruins relationships.

- Look out for the signs of aggressive behaviour in others and avoid using aggression yourself.

- Passive/non-assertive behaviour means being misunderstood or needs being ignored and therefore not met.

- Mentally rehearse assertive approaches using 'sound inner dialogues' – the self-talk that prepares for effective interactions between you and others.

- Use the three languages effectively.

- Don't be manipulated – clarify your rights in your own mind.

- Seek 'win-win' where needs are met and relationships strengthened.

Influencing

'The best way to persuade people is with your ears – by listening to them.'

Dean Rusk, former US Secretary of State

Good influencers get results but what a number of people who try to influence fail to recognise is that influence – unless it is done through the flexing of real immediate power ('I'm the boss') – is something that develops over time through the way you are with people, the results you get and the reputation you grow. There are several sources of influence for you. What sits right at the top is your own credibility. As has been said else-where your credibility will nearly always build up over time which is why 'reputation management' has become so popular. But you can't 'manage' your credibility or indeed your reputation. People see you as 'credible' when:

- They see you 'being' and 'doing' effectively – rather than saying what you are and what you are going to do.
- You are authentic – they see what they believe to be the real 'you' rather than the 'fake' you.

If all of this sounds rather like what makes people want to be led by a 'leader' then you are right and certainly the ability to influence is a primary characteristic of a good leader. A point made later (in the next chapter on working in a team) is that leadership is always conferred by those being led and it's not necessarily the team manager who will always take this role.

This influencing section of the chapter provides a 'walk-through' of the key influencing strategies available to you (e.g. forming coalitions for 'strength') and influencing strategies in different types of organisational cultures (e.g. with a very cen-tralised power base). This section also contains three worked examples of what to do in different situations in which influence is either needed or lacking. First, however, a reminder of what influencing is not. It is not a means of telling people what to do and expecting them to go off and do it. Good influencers live in the minds of those they seek to influence. They understand them and recognise that people will generally only do things with their hearts and heads when they understand what's in it for them.

 **example**

Here is a problem that I am asked about almost more than any other. It's a good example because it demonstrates a number of tools we can use as influencers:

Problem: *'I am initiating a new project in the team. How can I have influence when dealing with team colleagues who are much older than me, have more experience and have developed certain attitudes and behaviours.'*

There are two primary issues here. The first is building the credibility that a younger person will need in the eyes of older people. Of course, this is a requirement regardless of who you are trying to influence. The second is the approach you take to having influence over others (and not just older employees). Your mental rehearsal will be important once again as you prepare your approach to people.

Credibility takes time to build. Proving your skill/competence over time builds credibility like nothing else. Another tip is to emphasise your respect for others' wisdom and authority – but don't overdo it! Questions such as, 'I am trying to do xxxx. In your experience, what are the pitfalls, challenges, etc.'. Another way is to say, 'If you were in my shoes, using your experience, how would you go about it?' There is an old saying: if you want to instigate something that may meet with resistance, seek the GIFT ('Get It From Them'). You might not need to have the answers – or indeed any of them.

You don't want to be seen as threat. Doing things to make others look good (are there any 'quick wins' available?) without taking credit is one such way of achieving this.

There is also the 'question behind the question' here and, again it relates to influence. Can you find a way to influence people who have a set view of the world that can be hard to break?

Here, the WII FM – 'what's in it for me' – question can work. If people have developed set patterns of behaviour over time then they need good reasons to change that behaviour. Just because *you* see something as beneficial to others doesn't mean that they will. Force field analysis can help. In this method of analysis you make an assessment of the benefits of your proposed actions and rather than assuming that everyone will be delighted at this you make the assumption that that there will be resistance. Force field analysis allows you to establish where the resistance will reside and allows you to address those resistance factors. It's not that difficult to find out – just ask. By establishing the resistance factors you are now able to create a strategy for overcoming them should they occur.

Also, sometimes people just need to be heard. Do be seen to listen and empathise.

Influencing strategies

When influencing effectively we either consciously or subconsciously use particular strategies.

Trust

Trust should be the basis of effective working relationships and particularly so with your manager. If you are consistent, credible, honest, do what you say you are going to do, build on common ground and treat others reasonably and fairly then people will see you as trustworthy. Of course, abuse the trust and you lose it and it can take a long time to get it back again.

Your reputation

Your good reputation is an insurance policy. It gives you credibility particularly among those who might not know you well but know about you. People talk.

Logic

'If we don't do x then y will happen' or 'If we do this then it will benefit you because...' uses logical, reasoned argument as the source of influence. Logic can also answer the 'What's in it for me?' question we all have in our heads.

brilliant tip

Emphasising what you agree on - the shared ground - is a feature both of effective influencing and negotiation. To do this well you need to be clear on the needs and interests of the other person. We all have needs to be met and if you ignore the other person's needs (or don't even try to establish what they are) you may get your way once but it's no basis on which to develop a lasting relationship. The skills we looked at earlier apply here.

Coalition

Where one person is weak, many are strong. If you have a difficult issue to raise on which you want to secure agreement you would be wise to secure the support of those who agree with you *before* the meeting. Coalition has even been used with an intransigent manager, with team members collectively approaching the manager for a change of direction though this has to be done with great tact.

Doing a deal

'If you can do this for me I owe you one.'

brilliant tip

Reminding someone of your source of influence weakens it or even nullifies it. Saying 'Trust me' demands the response 'Why should I?' (when using trust as an influencing strategy) or saying, 'Remember how I helped you out last week? Well I need your help now' (when using 'doing a deal' as an influencing strategy) are examples of what not to say. Those being influenced decide how they will be influenced – if at all. While you can make reasonable assumptions about the approach that will work best for you these strategies should not be spelled out.

Influencing and culture

In his book *Understanding Organisations* Charles Handy identifies different organisational cultures. In this section we define the characteristics of three of these cultures – power, role, task-oriented – and suggest methods for influencing in each of those cultures. Think about the organisation you work for. How would you describe its culture? What strategies do you think might work best?

The power culture

A power culture is one in which a central source, perhaps even one person, dominates. Small entrepreneurial businesses can fit here and even in bigger organisations the thinking of one group or one person permeates everywhere. Partners in legal or accountancy firms may also comprise a very strong power source – almost feeling like an exclusive, tough-to-join club.

- The power source is easy to identify but not so easy to influence if you are on the outside.
- Build good relationships with those close to the power source such as advisers and PAs.
- Don't challenge the authority of the power source directly but use softer, strategic skills.
- Influence in a power culture comes from being noticed. Successes get you noticed and if they don't this is the

kind of environment in which it's good to blow your own trumpet from time to time.

The role culture

Role cultures often have pyramid structures with adherence to rules, tightly defined job roles and rigid 'performance management' systems. They thrive on planning and control which makes influence and change somewhat tougher. Their demise has been predicted for many years but over time many organisations take on this cultural form as a very long prelude to organisational death. That death can last many years or survival can be sustained through public funding which is why so many public-sector operations have these 'role culture' characteristics.

- Use clear, logical, systematic thinking that acknowledges internal systems and procedures.

- Big changes may work best if introduced incrementally or if big change is essential then building coalitions will be particularly important.

- Don't bulldoze your way up the hierarchy – potential supporters will become blockers very quickly.

- Identify ways in which you can work around the hierarchy. Extensive internal networking builds relationships in different parts of the business – develop your relationships into a spider's web of connected people (with you at the centre!) rather than just a linear hierarchy. Networks thrive on mutual support so do things for people without immediate expectation of favours in return.

Task-oriented culture

These cultures are flatter, more empowering and adaptable. They usually feature lots of project or self-managed teams. They work well in the good times. In the bad times they can change to more protectionist, survivalist 'role cultures'.

- You will have influence because of your capability and

reputation and not because of age, social status and experience.

- Because decision-making is made on a more consensual basis rather than purely as a result of seniority you can have more influence over the decision-making process.

- There is a greater scope for initiating projects – what we call 'intrapreneuring' – which means that your thoughts and ideas are more likely to be listened to.

- Just as reputations can be gained quickly they can be lost quickly too – these things work both ways – so pay attention to how you are being perceived. These cultures tend not to have many hiding places so they only suit certain kinds of people – task/results-driven ones.

brilliant impact

Even though the culture of an organisation will make influencing easier or more difficult, the biggest facilitator/barrier to influencing is your own perception of your level of influence. Take two people doing the same job – any job. One person will see no barrier in who he or she can influence, initiating conversation even with those at the top of the hierarchy. Another, in the same job will see their influence stretching no further than the narrow confines of the job. In fact, your capacity for influence starts as soon as you open your mouth and speak.

Putting it all together – assertiveness and influencing at a meeting

In this section some of the elements from assertiveness and its close cousin influencing are brought together into a coherent 'whole' – how you perform at meetings, which is something we spend a lot of time participating in (or not!) This continues the theme we first looked at earlier (in Chapter 3). A good guiding philosophy for you to follow is to say that assertive communication in meetings means saying what you want to say, appropriately, so that what you say is remembered by others, while listening to and respecting opinions that may not be the same as yours. This section is structured in three stages: preparation, performance and persistence.

Preparation

If you sometimes struggle to think on your feet in meetings, prepare ahead of time. Study the agenda, if there is one. Think what issues are likely to come up and what points you're likely to want to make. Then you'll be able to prepare and participate with maximum impact and effectiveness.

- **'What is my purpose here?'** What am I here for? Do I need to communicate a message or messages? To offer my opinion? To gather the views of others? To collectively problem-solve? Of course, you may be required to do all of these.

- Defining your role will help you be more effective – contributing more assertively – because you will prepare and perform better.

- Use **mental rehearsal** for the issues you want to raise – particularly for those issues that will stimulate debate. Refer back to the assertiveness section of this chapter which has several examples of how to construct 'sound inner dialogues'.

- **Coalitions**. One of the fears we have, 'I will be the only person who thinks like this'. Sound people out beforehand. Who feels the same way? Who will support you? Use influencing strategies such as trust and logical argument to win people over.

- **Scenario plan**. Ask what kind of questions/objections/ support you are likely to get. How will you react?

> ✹ **brilliant** tip
>
> We love to 'nest'. If you have regular meetings in the same room it's interesting how often people sit in the same places habitually, creating their own little 'safe' world. From time to time, for impact, try to sit somewhere different yourself.

Performance

- **The three languages.** Be clear in the way you express the points you want to raise (e.g. use simple language). Adopt the appropriate tone of voice for the message. This should be thought about in your preparation. If it's a very serious message then get the pitch right for a suitable level of gravity.

- **Check in with yourself.** Body language; posture; making eye contact when you speak; and using the minimal space around you (i.e. you are not rooted).

- **Support others**. If you want support from others, support them when they need it most.

- **Use 'I' and 'we' appropriately**. Use 'I' statements when expressing opinions rather than hiding behind others: 'I think that's an excellent idea' or 'As I see it, the problem is…'. Use 'we' when emphasising the common ground that exists between you and others.

- **Speak early for impact.** Speak as early as you can, certainly in the first five minutes. If you wait too long, you'll feel rising pressure for your contribution to be good – and may end up saying nothing at all.

- **Make connections**. Link what you say to what others have said. Just as you want your contributions to be remembered others want theirs to be as well. It's a great way to build coalitions with colleagues. Idea-building also does this – developing the ideas of others.

Persistence

- **Attract attention**. Introverts sometimes struggle to get their voice heard amidst the noise generated by the louder, more overtly opinionated types. Get the attention of the chairperson.

- **Use flattery**. If you need to get in and have your say try using flattery: 'That was a very interesting point', 'Can I stop you there because I want to explore that important point you've just made...' or 'I think that what you are saying is important. There is another way of looking at this'.

- **Pick your issues.** If you take an assertive stand on every issue you run the risk of being ignored. You might be seen as negative or awkward. Decide what is really important to you.

- **Avoid 'Yes but ...'.** If you want to interject avoid the conversation-killing '**YES**, it's an interesting idea **BUT** we can't do it because...' statement.

- **Follow up**. Follow up on issues raised and commitments made.

brilliant example

Problem: *'I have a problem. I am initiating a new project as part of a team but I am finding it difficult to secure cooperation from others. I need people to cooperate and they don't want to. I am struggling to influence them to see things my way and that there are benefits.'*

This needs a holistic approach. Why don't they want to cooperate? Have they seen it all before? Are they saying 'Here comes *another* initiative'? Why should they cooperate anyway? You have to find the real reasons behind the lack of cooperation – not just the superficial ones – before you find the solution.

There may be many reasons for people not wanting to cooperate but often there are two primary ones. First, that their needs have not been met in the potential solution. This means their needs as stated by them and not by you. Second, that they feel detached from the whole process and therefore have no sense of ownership of the solution. If a solution is imposed and/or it fails to address their needs then it is understandable that they may not wish to cooperate. Similarly if people feel they are being manipulated into a particular course of action they may well resent it. So, good advice in this situation is to, first, look at your own initial approach – back to your mental rehearsal and sound inner dialogue. Most people are reasonable if treated reasonably.

However, a few (very few) people are not reasonable. You can try to use 'coalition' tactics, gaining strength through the numbers of people who feel the same way as you, or you can see if you can bypass that particular person (this is used more often than we may think). However, we have to also understand that difficult people are a part of life and sometimes we just have to work 'round' them rather than through them.

brilliant recap

- Building trust, being credible and building a good reputation give you influence.
- Influence doesn't mean you ignore the wants and needs of others. Almost everyone asks the 'WII FM' question.
- Influencing features many of the core elements we associate with assertiveness (e.g. excellent communication skills, good mental rehearsal).
- Building on common ground creates a way forward.
- Consciously adopt the correct influencing strategy for the person and the situation (e.g. 'coalition' when you are individually weak).
- Adapt your approach for different organisational cultures.

CHAPTER 7

Working in a team

'It is literally true that you can succeed best and quickest by helping others to succeed.'

Napoleon Hill, author

One of the biggest changes in organisations over the past 20–30 years has been the strong shift towards team-working with words such as 'collaboration' and phrases such as 'self-managed teams' now common linguistic currency in effectively run organisations. A good example is the way in which we create, innovate and problem-solve. Historically, in North American and North European organisations, there was the idea of the 'great man' who would emerge with the new idea, the breakthrough, the invention (this in an era of few women in senior roles). Learning from efficient team-working and collaborative practices that emerged from successful post-war economies such as Germany and Japan many organisations adopted some of the team-working techniques that had proved to be so successful there. Of course we have always had team-working. However, there has never been a time when it has been so central to the functioning of organisations. A lot of thought and effort is put into team composition, team motivation and team resourcing of teams.

Within this there have been three primary shifts that affect us as team-workers. The first is the move towards what are known as 'self-managed' teams – semi-autonomous and responsible for setting goals and the day-to-day work agenda. This shift is ongoing in many organisations and features in project teams for example. The second is that the teams are far less hierarchical than has historically been the case. The third is that teams are likely to operate remotely using online tools to communicate effectively. This third development is covered later (see the final chapter). These changes affect anyone who works in teams. Specifically:

- team members are valued for what they individually bring to the team in terms of knowledge, skills and behaviour
- the team may not be as formally 'led' as it was in the past. Although there is likely to a designated coordinator/ manager/leader there will be opportunities for other members to provide leadership in certain situations much in the way that a football team doesn't just have a captain but also leaders in defence, midfield and attack
- a more egalitarian approach means that interpersonal skills that support collaboration, consensus, problem-solving, decision-making and goal-setting (among other things) are now even more valuable than they were in the past

With all this in mind the purpose of this chapter is to look at three areas of team-working:

- your 'role' in the team
- collaborative behaviour (using creative problem-solving as an example)
- when the team meets.

In each case the intention is not to look in general terms at how teams operate but, rather, how you can be at your most effective and impactful in a team context.

brilliant tip

Confucius once said that 'at the feast of ego, everyone leaves hungry'. Brilliant teams harness the talents and uniqueness of each team member so that what comes out is greater than the sum of its parts – that is, greater than that which would occur if each team member was acting in isolation. While individualism and uniqueness are valued the toxicity of overactive egos damages the team greatly. Be yourself but do it for positive ends. For example, you can be a sceptic at times but there is a big difference between constructive (aiming for improvement) and destructive (aiming to damage) scepticism.

Your role in the team

There are two groups of roles that team members need to perform so that a team works effectively. These are technical roles and team roles.

Technical roles

The 'technical roles' relate to the specific nature of the work being done. They will depend on individual knowledge and expertise and may even require formal qualifications if they are to be performed effectively. You may be employed because you have that specific expertise. Applying your knowledge and skills will therefore be one way in which you contribute to the work of the team.

Team roles

 brilliant definition

A **team role** is 'a tendency to behave, contribute and interrelate with others in a particular way', said Meredith Belbin, a team role expert.

'Team roles' relate particularly to behavioural preferences you and your colleagues display individually as the team goes about its work. Extensive research (see Belbin (2010) and Honey (2001)) has thrown up a number of team roles that should be performed in almost all teams. These have been synthesised into seven core team roles, listed below, combining the name for the team role together with the behaviour/contribution linked to the role:

- **leaders/coordinators** – Direction
- **drivers** – Action
- **creators** – Ideas
- **harmonisers** – Relationships
- **achievers** – Results
- **challengers** – Restraint
- **networkers** – Resources.

So, as an ideal, these sound sensible. An effective team needs to know where it is going); it needs energetic, active people; it needs fresh thinking; it needs someone to act as the 'emotional glue' in the team, maintaining strong relationships; it needs to achieve its goals; it needs a brake against ill-thought-through decisions and action; and it needs people who connect the team with the world beyond it. It's hard to argue against these roles being needed in any workplace and it's also hard to argue against any of them being critical to team effectiveness.

So, what does this mean for you? First you need to establish which role suits you best. A key consideration is that although all these roles need to be performed in an effective team it is unlikely that you perform only one of them. The likelihood is that two, or perhaps even three, are a natural fit for you. In addition it is likely that other colleagues in the team perform more than one role effectively and that the behavioural preferences that others have will overlap with your own. It may also be the case that one or two roles have to be performed by team members even if the role doesn't come particularly naturally to any one team member. At times that will mean you have to do this.

brilliant tip

Playing your part in the effective performance of the team is important, but all of us have a tendency to see the world through our own eyes, accentuating the value that we bring to the world – in this case the team. Each role is of equal value and without the performance of each role the team's performance dips. Appreciate that although you have your role(s) to play, others play equally important roles as well.

For each role we will look at what it involves and the benefits the role brings to the team – and you can think about how you behave and interact in your team and what roles or roles you naturally gravitate towards. As noted, are likely to have more than one but no more than three. We will also look at the strengths of each role but also its vulnerabilities. Vulnerability is a better word than 'weakness' because weakness implies that a particular behavioural characteristic is to be avoided all the time. The word 'vulnerability' means that a behaviour has an important place, but that it also can be damaging in certain situations. For example, stubbornness can be an asset when applied to ill-thought-through plans that might land the team with problems but it can be frustrating when the team is in a fast-moving situation and needs to act quickly.

As you read through these roles think about your own behaviour. What have you brought to teams that you have been involved in over the past few years? What roles fit most naturally with you?

The roles

If you are a leader/coordinator

The leader/coordinator should be able to recognise the value of the behavioural and knowledge-based contributions of team members and bring them to the fore appropriately. Critically, however, the leader/coordinator will create a vision, direction or purpose and keep us working towards team goals. The coordinator is particularly important in relation to keeping the team goal-focused and concentrating on the systems and procedures that will get the team there.

If you are a designated or non-designated leader

A manager is formally appointed. The leader is the person whom the rest of the group gravitate towards for direction – particularly vision – and perhaps also inspiration. That means *anyone* is potentially the leader of the team, even temporarily. You can become a leader because of at least some of the following: your specialist knowledge and skills in a particular area; your experience and credibility; your 'empathic' approach; your sense of 'direction' for the team; and your charisma. In addition, technological 'savvy' also draws people towards those who have it (because most of us really want it!). For some it will be because of all of these. Leaders typically operate on either a supportive, consensual basis (a more people-centred approach to getting the group to move in a particular direction) or on a directive basis ('This is where we are going, this is how we are going to get there'). Both are equally important. In some situations the role performed is more of a coordinating one rather than a leadership role. The coordinator looks after the processes and procedures that help the team achieve its goals.

There is a contemporary saying that goes 'When it is necessary to lead, then lead. When it is necessary to be led, then be led.' This implies emotional maturity on your part in that when a team member moves into a position where their behavioural and technical skills are needed to provide direction and focus for the group (and they have credibility in the role) then your ego should be calmed so you don't see this ad hoc movement into a leadership role as a challenge to you. There is nothing that affects team effectiveness more than groups of competing egos.

Strengths

Without direction or purpose most action is meaningless. Without thinking through the steps necessary to achieve team goals, those goals are merely pipedreams. As a leader/coordinator your strength is keeping the team goal-centred.

Vulnerabilities

Leadership and coordination can be done in different ways and, if you find yourself in this role you should be aware of your own personal style as authenticity is important – be true to yourself. We have already referred to 'supportive' and 'directive' approaches to leadership. There are others. The vulnerability you have as a leader/coordinator comes from using the wrong leadership style with a particular person or in a particular situation. Adapt your style to the person and the situation. Another book in the series, *Brilliant Teams*, looks at the styles available in detail.

If you are a driver

Strengths

As a driver you provide an initial impetus – the 'can-do' attitude – that teams need when they are working on new ideas and initiatives. The driver is the one who says 'I'll drive' when a car journey needs to be made and this is the team equivalent of that. Sound familiar? You are good at seeing the reasons for doing things first (before the reasons for inaction) and people can be inspired by the positive attitude you display.

As a driver you also have a real 'intrapreneurial' streak. Intrapreneurs are the employed version of entrepreneurs. You like putting new ideas into action.

Vulnerabilities

If you are a driver don't be put off by the number of vulnerabilities below.

- Drivers can be so fast-moving that people can't keep up – significant when you need the support of the team. Don't leave things 'half done' because the next thing is more exciting.

- Do you have a road map? Drivers do lots of things but do you do the right things? As we shall see with another of the roles there is a difference between 'doing' and 'achieving'.

- In your desire for action, if things get quiet, you may embark on ill-considered action.

- Being task-orientated is great but 'ways and means' are important too (e.g. working in financial services post-2007).

brilliant tip

Because 'doers' are associated with action they might not admit when they are struggling. If this is you, there is no shame in asking for help when confronted with possible heroic failure.

If you are a creator

As a creator you are the idea generator and the potential problem-solver in the team. You may be voluble but equally as a creator you may well be thoughtful and contemplative. You act as a 'team helicopter' hovering above a situation, making an assessment of that situation and considering a range of possible alternatives to deal with it.

Strengths

As well as having ideas, the creator should be good at building on the ideas of others. Many teams satisfy themselves with a limited number of new ideas or allow good initial ideas to remain under-developed and as a fresh thinker you can develop these ideas.

Vulnerabilities

If you are at the contemplator/thinker end of the creativity scale, don't hide your thoughts. A good leader will recognise this and draw your thoughts out but don't rely on that happening. You have insights and thoughts that are of immense value so do try to come forward. (Chapter 6 on assertiveness will help if this is an issue for you.)

As a creator you see 'the bigger picture'. However, you may get lost in your thoughts and, as a consequence, you may get stuck in the minutiae – and then struggle to break out from that more limited perspective.

New thinking can be a game with no end. At some point ideas and options need to be moved on into action.

If you are a harmoniser

You are concerned with the preservation of good relationships within your group. Of all of the roles this is the one that is the most undervalued (being seen by some as a bit 'soft and fluffy'). This role has the same value as the others but it is tempting to say that 'ideas' (creators) and 'action' (achievers, doers) are more important because they are more tangible and add more obvious and visible value. Your role as a harmoniser is tough to perform but essential to the wellbeing of the team.

Strengths

You generate team cohesion by working at ensuring good rela-tionships between team members. Your role is often a subtle, less obvious one. But it is a critical one. Teams need emotional glue – a binding that keeps them together through the challenges, the conflicts, the disagreements and the stresses of day-to-day working. Because 'harmonisers' are emotionally and socially intelligent you sense what the 'emotional climate' is within the team and can iron out problems, then use the skills we associate with this, such as listening, empathy and mediation.

Vulnerabilities

In the desire for team accord the harmonisers might feel the need to harmonise even in situations that have aroused only slight disagreement. If this is you then reflect that a little creative, constructive tension in the team can be a good thing. Harmonising becomes valuable, however, when the disagreement becomes destructive.

If you are an achiever

As we saw, a driver is concerned with action but there is no guarantee that he or she will achieve the right things. As an achiever you do just that. You help the team meet its goals because you focus on deadlines and results. You check the detail, often have a direct, no-nonsense style and use failure as a spur to future success. You may be a 'quiet' achiever but those who know the work of the team know the work you do for it.

Strengths

You are in the results business. You get results. Because of your attention to detail, you recognise the need for systems and procedures and you are willing to pick up the administrative shortfall.

Vulnerabilities

As an achiever you are likely to be aware of your value. This means you might not be great at sharing or delegating. This may come from the need for control. This need for control can cause stress if you feel loss of control and that stress can easily permeate the team if it's not managed. Some achievers nag others because they are driven to finish work and this can create tension. Not everyone works in the same way as you and you need to curb your frustration.

 **tip**

Achievers attend to the detail, but not everyone shares this focus. Be prepared to think through the way you approach people explaining why you need certain things (e.g. an extra set of figures, or an additional proofread of an important document). Remember SPARC. People need to understand the 'why' of requested action – the purpose.

If you are a challenger

As a challenger you are analytical, weighing up the options and sounding warnings when potential action has been ill-thought-through. A driver, in particular can find this frustrating and, as a consequence you might not be the most popular member of the team, but, if this is you, you may not be too bothered by this!

Strengths

You are good at playing the devil's advocate role. You look at problems in different ways and ask, 'How would x see this?' or 'Can we look at this in a different way?'

You have high standards, searching for continuous improvement and you are the natural quality controller in a team. You bring the benefit of strategic thinking, planning ahead and thinking through the consequences of actions beyond the short term.

Vulnerabilities

Does everything need to be perfect? Are there times when 'good enough is good enough'? There are times when the pursuit of perfection isn't necessary – Facebook for example uses the motto 'done is better than perfect'. Be judicious about what and when you challenge.

In the next section on collaboration, we look at how to challenge ideas without damaging relationships or killing creativity. This can be a vulnerability for challengers, who are prone to using 'Yes, but ...'-type statements.

If you are a networker

As a networker you are a valuable member of the team but a lot of your work is done beyond the team. You work around traditional hierarchies, building relationships with people throughout your organisation. You are in touch with the 'political' climate, in tune with gossip and trends. You are a good communicator and inclined to extraversion, though certainly not always – contacts are often built up in more subtle ways.

Strengths

Teams often slip into silo mentality – separating the work they do from other teams, the organisation as a whole and the world outside. As a networker you are valuable in connecting the team to the world beyond the team, reminding team members that they cannot operate in isolation.

You bring resources, contacts and new thinking. Your work may extend beyond the organisation to customers, suppliers and even competitors.

You are an ambassador for the team and you have the interpersonal skills that can show the work of the team.

You identify opportunities for the team.

Vulnerabilities

Networkers can be random in outlook and you need to filter out what isn't useful from what is. If you are a natural networker allow the challengers in because they can do this. Don't treat them as a threat or take objective comments personally.

The randomness does also mean sometimes moving from one thing to another and leaving others to pick up the pieces.

Networking is a randomised activity because you can't know which connections have value and which don't. Treat networking as an altruistic rather than a self-seeking activity. The 'users' soon get spotted.

 **brilliant** recap

- Team members need to fullfil a number of key roles – technical and behavioural – that need to be performed.
- The seven key behavioural roles are: leader/coordinator, driver, creator, harmoniser, achiever, challenger, and networker.
- You will have at least one behavioural role type that comes more naturally to you than others – possibly up to three although in rare cases more.
- Use the strengths of the role type for the benefit of the team.
- Be aware that most role types also come with potential vulnerabilities that affect the team's output.

Collaborative behaviour

brilliant definition

Collaboration is an approach that optimises human interaction so that the output of that interaction is exponentially superior to the contribution any one person would make in isolation of another person or group. Collaboration makes 1 + 1 = 3.

In this section we will look at the way in which you can maximise your effectiveness as a collaborator and not just as a contributor to the team. Many of the behaviours that feature here have been covered earlier (in Chapter 5) and you will find it useful to refer back to that chapter when 'listening', for example, is mentioned here, for a reminder of what listening really is – a means to truly rather than superficially understand.

 **example**

Collaborative advantage

Here is an interesting way in which organisations see the need for collaboration. In the old days organisations used to talk about 'competitive advantage'. In this new hyper-connected age organisations now talk about 'collaborative advantage'. What does that mean? In one industry sector, pharmaceutical companies have historically been very secretive about what they do, keeping trial data hidden and fiercely protecting patents. The industry isn't about to open itself up to the world but one pharmaceutical company, GSK, has made much of its trial data freely available recognising that we've moved from a model of keeping your secrets close to your chest giving you competitive advantage to one of competitive advantage coming from collaborative advantage. By making information available GSK invites people from outside its inner sanctum to connect, contribute, collaborate and also, of course, criticise through online connectivity. Many see this collaborative openness as *the* key way of maintain competitive advantage in the future.

This isn't just a phenomenon within hi-tech industries. In the UK, post-crash budgetary cuts have meant that organisations in the public sector, such as local councils and authorities, are sharing resources and collaborating to present tendering opportunities to suppliers collectively rather than as isolated units. This brings significant savings.

So, for you, in your team role, collaboration might not mean just within the team but also beyond the team – the reason that the 'networkers' identified in the previous section on team roles are so important. In this section we will look at the skills we associate with true collaboration and in the following section the forum where collaboration usually happens – team meetings.

Collaboration – where it goes wrong/what you can do right

Collaboration occurs when there is the need to solve a problem or identify and make the most of an opportunity. You may know the saying that 'problems are opportunities' and that has some truth to it. However, lots of teams don't really understand what collaboration means. Here we look at how you can play your role as an effective collaborator but will do so in a way that helps acknowledge the problems teams have in understanding what collaboration involves.

The vague goal

There is no point in collaborating if there is nothing to collaborate about. Most teams get this but still often set a goal that is vague, doesn't solve the real problem or, most importantly of all, fails to inspire. You must feel there is an incentive to collaborate – we solve 'X' problem, or take 'Y' opportunity. The team that can capture the problem or opportunity in its collective mind also has the solution.

Your effectiveness as a team member will be maximised if you help the team work out the real heart of a problem so that the goal can be clearly defined.

How? Problems and opportunities – and the goal we therefore set as a team to solve the problem or develop the opportunity – are identified through evidence and gut feeling. As part of the team you have access to evidence that will help the team define the goal clearly. The evidence can be statistical: 'We have only sold three of "X" product in the last three months. In the same period last year we sold 25.' It could be anecdotal: 'I have had three customers tell me that if we could respond in 24 hours instead of 48 they would give us more business.' Your knowledge, and the sharing of this knowledge comes from really tuning in to your job.

Big goal, small steps

Earlier (in Chapter 4) we saw that there is research which concludes, while a big goal can be motivating what really gets us started is the small steps we take along the way. Sometimes the goal just seems too big. If you have ever moved house the packing-up operation can seem daunting, but first you pack the kitchen stuff, then the books, then your clothes and suddenly you're on your way. If you are meeting a goal then bite-size pieces is the way to go.

Your effectiveness as a team member will be maximised if you can encourage your colleagues through your own behaviour, to think small to get big results.

How? Thoughts and ideas often come out half-formed and need to be developed, but some of us seem programed to look for the faults in the suggestion (the 20 per cent of it that is bad) right away as though there is nothing good to be had. Remember that behaviour breeds behaviour. If one or two people start acting in this way others either clam up ('What's the point in contributing?') or start mirroring the same behaviour.

Ego masks

These occur when team members forget that they are trying to solve a problem or create an opportunity and treat what should be a collaborative exercise as a competitive sport – 'My idea is better than your idea', or 'Here's the reason your idea won't work'. In the worst cases there is a fight for power as some team members believe themselves to be superior to others. The rest leave them to it and stop contributing.

Your effectiveness as a team member will be maximised if you can make regular contributions and acknowledge that the contributions of others are equally valid.

How? Ego – the mask we hide behind – is amplified in group situations, but ego is actually a contaminant that denies the real you to yourself. Deepak Chopra puts it very well:

There is only one answer

'The ego, however, is not who you really are. The ego is your self-image; it is your social mask; it is the role you are playing. Your social mask thrives on approval. It wants control, and it is sustained by power, because it lives in fear.'

Deepak Chopra, author

There are a few problems that have just one or very few answers. We call these 'cognitive' problems. In our formative years through education we are trained to think that there is the 'single right answer' to most problems. In truth however, most problems have a variety of possible solutions. Indeed, some believe that only mathematics is fact, everything else is opinion.

While that may be extreme, your effectiveness as a team member will be maximised if you can stretch your thinking. Creativity expert Roger Von Oech, says we should think in terms of there being 'the first right answer, the second right answer, the third right answer...' and so on.

How? By stretching your own thinking and encouraging others to stretch theirs. See below under 'Lack of ideas' for more on this. One reason for this is that we don't give ourselves 'time to think'. A great way to do this is to 'prime' your own thinking – that is, prepare yourself to make a contribution well in advance of when you need to collaborate and contribute (see the 'Brilliant impact' next).

↗ brilliant impact

Using the 'mental dimmer switch' is a good way to create new ideas – it can fundamentally affect the impact you have at team meetings. You cannot idle your way to insight but equally 'forcing yourself to think' – wrestling with problems, opportunities, challenges and conundrums – without giving your brain time to think is counterproductive. Control the mental dimmer switch so the thinking light is low but not switched off. We don't completely understand how this works, but, while the conscious mind is working on something the 'undermind' will be 'playing' with something else – quite possibly your problem or opportunity. The 'undermind' doesn't seem to work so well when we force it to, so the key here is to start playing with ideas in your own mind well in advance of when the team will next be together. So give your 'undermind' a chance to do its best work. This explains why many people say they get their best ideas in the shower, on a bike, when swimming or even on the toilet. The 'undermind' has been 'at play' even though we weren't aware of it. It's excellent for team brainstorming. Simply by aware of the brainstorming topic in advance so you can make use of your formidable brain to its best advantage.

Lack of ideas

Most future thinkers agree that innovation is one of the central battlegrounds for organisations that want to thrive. However, research by innovation think tank the Dolphin Organisation concludes that what's missing most in teams is a lack of fresh thinking. Teams identify problems, make decisions about solving those problems and then act but the numbers of ideas they generate to solve the problem are typically fairly limited. This is particularly true if the team has been together for a while – it acts on a dwindling number of fresh ideas.

Your effectiveness as a team member will be maximised if you can offer new thinking and explore your creative capability.

How? Learn to think in multiple ways – routine thinking, evolutionary thinking and revolutionary thinking.

Routine thinking

Routine thinking is the instinctive realm we have for ideas because it's both familiar and safe. Convention is fine in many situations, so we go for the things we already do and are comfortable with. We may tweak things a little but there's no breakthrough thinking here. As a team member you will be valuable if you can think in new, fresh ways, but equally you shouldn't do this to the exclusion of the obvious and conventional. However, don't get *stuck* in the routine. We all have a remarkable capacity for creating new ideas if we learn to fully engage with a problem or opportunity.

brilliant tip

In routine thinking it is accepted that 'the way we do it' is a helpful mind-set. But it can also be a prison that stops us from looking at problems in new ways. As you move in to evolutionary and revolutionary thinking you will find it helpful to say to yourself, 'The way we *don't* do it' as a catalyst for asking, 'How can this problem be solved in a different way?', 'Who can we learn from?' or, 'What are our competitors doing that we have barely noticed or just chosen to ignore?'

Evolutionary thinking

Evolutionary thinking occurs when you make a link between similar things that share some characteristics and apply one to the other. They do not require huge leaps of creative imagination but they require a step forward from convention. It may be that you observe what other organisations do that aren't operating in your industry. A few years ago only 'tech' companies would tweet. Now it's almost essential for all companies to be 'followed'.

 **tip**

A good question to ask is 'Who has their version of our problem and how did they solve it?'

Revolutionary thinking

Revolutionary thinking can occur when you make connections between things that on the surface, at least, do not have any connection. Have you ever eaten 'Cherry Garcia' ice-cream from Ben and Jerry's? Here the manufacturers chose not to name the flavour of the ice-cream after the ingredients (routine thinking). Instead they named it after a rock star – a 1960s performer with the rock band 'The Grateful Dead', Jerry Garcia who just happened to be a favourite of Ben and Jerry's.

Good revolutionary thinking can also occur when you ask questions such as, 'What can't be done, but if it could, would fundamentally change the way we do things?' or 'What is it impossible to do in our industry now?' Ask these questions and then work backwards – it's amazing how quickly the impossible becomes realisable.

brilliant tip

Can you learn from people who operate in different walks of life to your own? What could a town planner learn from a brain surgeon who understands the ruts, grooves and gullies of the human brain? What could a shopping centre designer learn from a walk in a forest just after it has rained? Some of this might sound 'weird', but what's weird today is convention tomorrow.

Lack of listening

We can tell when people aren't listening in the team. They interrupt, use that tell-tale phrase, 'Yes, but...' (was there ever a bigger idea killer?), kill the thoughts and ideas of others, try to dominate rather than contribute and through facial gestures in particular reveal what they are really thinking and feeling about others and their thoughts.

Your effectiveness as a team member will be maximised if you can listen creatively (see Chapter 5) as an aid to collaboration.

How? Ask for more – help people develop their own thoughts ('That's interesting, tell us more'). Build on the thoughts and ideas of others – 'That's an interesting idea, we could take that initial idea and then...' or 'I like the thinking, we could...'. We call this 'idea piggy-backing' – taking the essence of a thought or idea and improving it.

Partial presence

This is so common. You see it in the form of late arrival, distractedness (gadget fiddling in particular), negative or closed body language and lack of contribution. It's also typical of those who overly value themselves (or undervalue others) that they tune out if it's not their turn to speak or they don't see others as credible or their contribution as valuable. Your effectiveness in the team will be maximised if you bring your 'whole' self to the team at all times.

How? Bringing your whole self means preparing for team meetings, contributing fully, supporting others, listening properly, 'checking in' with your physical behaviour, leaving the toys alone – that includes not taking calls and checking emails – and being seen to have done the things you have committed to.

 recap

- Many organisations see the art of collaboration as a key competitive advantage.
- Collaboration means the output exceeds the collective contributions of individuals in the team – we take the combined thinking to another level of performance altogether.
- Collaboration solves problems and creates and exploits opportunities.
- Have a big goal but tackle it step-by-step.
- Avoid contaminating the collaborative process with an overactive ego.
- Nearly all problems have many solutions. Nearly all opportunities have many way in which they can be exploited.
- You have a wonderful capacity for idea generation – use routine, evolutionary and revolutionary thinking.
- Listen to and build on the thinking of others.
- Bring your whole self to the team – mind, body and spirit.

When the team meets

'Every meeting that does not stir the imagination and curiosity of attendees and increase bonding and cooperation and engagement and sense of worth and motivate and enhance enthusiasm is a permanently lost opportunity.'

Tom Peters, business guru

One key forum for collaboration is the team meeting – notice how the quote above uses those powerful words, 'bonding', 'cooperation' and 'engagement', all key elements within effective collaboration. We've all sat through long, poorly run meetings.

Sometimes it's an 'ego show' dominated by two or three of the louder participants. Sometimes you sit wondering why you're even there when only one or two agenda issues concern you. Sometimes it feels like a 'meeting for the sake of having a meeting'. You may not be in a position to influence the format, timing and efficient running of a meeting but you can control how you prepare and perform so that you are a part of the collaborative process. Earlier (in Chapter 6) we looked in more detail at your performance in relation to more challenging issues such as an opinion you wish to express about which there is likely to be disagreement. In the previous section, we looked at some of the barriers to collaboration and what you can do as a team member to overcome them. In this section we look at key things that you can control and which will ensure you maximise your effectiveness as a contributor and collaborator at every team meeting. Some of the suggestions build on what's been said in the previous section.

Your preparation

- Meetings don't just happen to you – you 'happen' to a meeting.
- *Read the previous minutes*. Particularly applicable if it is a regular meeting – have you done what you committed to?
- *Know why you are there*. What is your expected contribution? If it's not a regular meeting ask what your contribution is expected to be and if you are required to be there for the whole meeting or part of it. Think through the points you want to raise, and if any are sensitive, the appropriate way of raising them.
- *Read any written material beforehand.* It is a horrible feeling when others have done this and you haven't or when you make a point that you would have known had been covered if you had done your pre-meeting reading.

- *Taking notes.* Yes, it's obvious but it's amazing how many people turn up to meetings without pen and paper.

Your timing

- If you haven't met some of the participants before, be a little early so that you can have a brief chat before the start – even if it's just to introduce yourself.

- *Keep to* your *own time* – if you have 10 minutes allocated don't take 15. No one will thank you for overrunning. In fact they may not even be listening if it's lunchtime or the end of the day.

- Team time belongs to the team – no distractions.

Your presence when others are contributing

These points are particularly important when collaborating because it isn't just about you. You want to encourage others. You need to signal your interest and engagement with other team members. You must however, be sincere. Here's a reminder of what's been said elsewhere (see also 'Your language' below).

- Maintain eye contact with the speaker, perhaps smile at the right moment.

- Nod your head to indicate that you are listening.

- Make affirmative noises – even just an 'mmm' will do.

brilliant tip

Making notes shows you are *really* interested in what the other person is saying. You are sending a signal: 'This is interesting. I want to remember it. I will write it down'.

Your language

Calibrate and regulate your own behaviour through the use of the three languages: language (words), paralanguage (tone) and body language. (Refer back to Chapter 5 for a reminder of the key points.)

- *Paralanguage* – talking a touch louder and a touch slower than you would in normal conversation at certain points gets people listening to you. If you have something to say, ensure it can be heard. Vary the pace.
- *Body language* – keep your head 'up' otherwise your voice 'drops' and your body and the palms of your hands 'open'.
- *Language* – meetings can shift between the formal and informal but you should keep to the point. In collaboration there should be minimal use of 'I' and much more 'we'. In the following section we will look at the words to use in collaborative processes such as problem-solving and idea-generation.

Your courteousness

This is important when, for example, you are interrupted. Have a couple of phrases you can use (and a bit of flattery can help too). People like to have their voices heard but it can be to the detriment of what you want to say, so say, for example:

- 'Let me just finish this bit, then I'll come back to that point'
- 'That's an interesting point. I've just got a couple more things to say and then I will answer it.'

Your action

Meetings, unless they are formal team briefings, should be a call to action, a decision-making forum and you should play your part. Commit to what you can realistically commit to and make sure that your action points and deadlines are recorded in the minutes – it's very difficult to recall this a few days later.

Getting involved now means you will be an active part of the next meeting rather than an observer.

 **tip**

Retrospectively raising issues after meetings (a 'no') shouldn't preclude 'lobbying' and creating coalitions before meetings – a crucial part of influencing. If you need to present an issue at a meeting that is controversial or about which there will be disagreement, gaining strength through alliances with others beforehand will strengthen your hand. (This is a topic covered more substantially in Chapter 6.)

Your goals

What goals do you have personally for the meeting? Do you want to influence the group to see the validity of your view or to take a particular course of action? Do you want to take the chance to hear what's really going on – office politics as well as strategic plans? Perhaps you are looking forward to discussing new opportunities. If you want to make an impact, influence people and be part of effective decision-making then practise skills such as speaking/presenting to groups and assert yourself as there are few better environments for doing so. Meetings get criticised and often rightly so but they provide a great opportunity for your own professional development.

brilliant recap

- Happen to a meeting – don't let it happen to you.
- Engage with the team.
- Be multilingual – speak language, paralanguage and body language.
- Exhibit good manners.
- Meetings provide excellent learning opportunities in relatively non-threatening environments.

PART 3

How to make a virtual impact

CHAPTER 8

Working in a virtual world

'Technology is the campfire around which we tell our stories.'

Laurie Anderson, performance artist and musician

Online connectivity, VoIP (Voice over Internet Protocol), client portals, email, collaborative networks, LinkedIn, video conferencing and virtual or remote teams have all appeared in the world of work over the past 20 years. They have created their own challenges (has there ever been a bigger timewaster than the misuse of email?) but they have transformed the way we work, communicate, create and collaborate. In some ways things are not so different. The email we now get used to live in the in tray (and the in-tray was always full). In other ways, however, they are very different.

In this chapter we are going to look at three aspects of contemporary working life in its 'virtual' form. The first is working in a remote or virtual team. The second is online 'social networking' and we look at how to use it, in particular to maximise your online impact. LinkedIn is the reference point though other networking tools such as Yammer offering connectivity and collaborative opportunities are key parts of the networking mix. Many of the rules of effective online social networking are shared across many of the networking tools available. The third element is an issue we looked at earlier (in Chapter 3) – the use and misuse of emails. Here, there is an emphasis on how to communicate effectively with it. There is some debate as to whether email as we know and love it will exist in ten years' time. Right now however, it is our primary communication tool, other than the spoken word, in working life.

Although we may not always be physically together the idea of great team-working has become more important, not less. The need for those core skills we associate with great teams such as excellent communication and focused collaboration is amplified when the team meets irregularly, if at all. However, it's not just about whether teams meet regularly or irregularly. It's also about how so much of the team's work is done away from the team regardless of how often they meet.

Remote and virtual teams

If you've worked as part of a remote team – increasingly many of us are doing so even if it's only part of the time – you may already be familiar with the some of the challenges that physical separation generates. Intercultural consultancy RW3 conducted a study on virtual teams recently and found that the majority of respondents, unsurprisingly, found decision-making, dealing with disagreement/conflict and the ease with which opinions could be expressed that much harder in virtual/remote teams. Close to a majority also found delivering quality work and creativity (e.g. generating new ideas) that much harder too. You may find that some of your challenges include:

- a feeling of 'separateness' including disconnection from what's going on
- keeping a sense of purpose and goal focus'
- keeping lines of communication open when rarely (if ever) meeting face-to-face – misunderstandings can be the consequence
- collaboration and sharing ideas, which can be harder if we are geographically dispersed.

So, in this section we cover four areas that reflect these challenges:

1 working in isolation

2 maintaining purpose

3 virtual communication

4 effective relationships online relationships.

1. Working in isolation

Feeling isolated when working in a virtual team or working from home is an understandable issue but such is the availability of different platforms for increased connectivity that the problem is largely self-inflicted. It does require proactivity on your part. While some of the networking platforms we mention later in this chapter keep you in touch with the wider world there is a need to keep in touch with team members and to push yourself forward a little more than you would in an office environment. Keeping in touch with your manager to update him or her on what you're doing is important but keeping in touch also allows you to know what's going on. Don't wait to hear from your manager or team colleagues – be the first to make contact if you are starting to feel left out. So, this is the start point – your proactive approach is needed to keep in touch with others and to let them know what you are doing.

One way that isolation affects us in particular is in problem-solving. As already mentioned, collaboration is such an important element in problem-solving so:

- make use of your employer's online collaborative platforms if you have them for idea generation
- make use of external platforms for sharing ideas (though do be aware of corporate confidentiality matters)
- join groups where the participants share working practices

that are similar to your own – you can use this as a support network if you need to.

2. Maintaining purpose

As we saw earlier (in Chapter 4) goals are important as a source of motivation for you personally but they are also important for teams, and especially remote teams, as a unifying force. Keep reminding yourself what the core focus of your work is – what's it meant to be achieving, what's it delivering? – as this is what will make you most effective as a remote team member.

If distance is a communication barrier, then not only is the goal important but so is a clear understanding of your role in delivering it. What does the team expect of you?

When you make demands of others share the purpose with them – 'You doing this helps me to…' – because, as we also saw earlier, purpose is a prime element in feeling engaged. If you want people to do things for you to the best of their ability then be clear about the reasons for them needing to do so.

3. Virtual communication

A point that has been made throughout this book is that while you can only influence others the one thing you can control and take responsibility for is your own self. This point is accentuated in virtual team-working and in particular, responsibility for communication. One of the biggest weaknesses in virtual teams is the differences in the level of knowledge of the tools and platforms that make virtual team-working easier between team members. A priority for you if you spend time working remotely is to take the opportunities to develop your knowledge of, for example, platforms that allow for effective online collaboration and for sharing ideas within the team and beyond it. For example, using client portals to share information and collaborate with clients is great but if the knowledge of how to use the client portal (or any other kind of facility) is limited to a few people then immediately there is a problem.

'In touch'

If you have a team coordinator keep him or her updated with your diary – don't wait to be asked or be slow to update. Some organisations make this process easier by having electronic diaries accessible to everyone but there will be times when a quick call or personal email breaks the monotony of the 'colder' methods of keeping in touch. It also creates energy (which is often very hard to feel in a disparate team) when you make the effort to connect through 'inter-human' rather than 'inter-net' methods.

brilliant tip

Workers in virtual teams may often keep unconventional hours – particularly those who work from home. Do be considerate. Just because you are hard at it at 9.30 p.m. on a Friday doesn't mean that others will appreciate an email or a phone call asking for a quick response.

Share your success stories, what's not going so well, market information, client feedback – whatever will interest colleagues. Online noticeboards, intranets and collaborative tools bring people closer but they only do so when they are used consistently and kept up-to-date. Just as we have seen that isolation can be a struggle for you, this applies to others too, so keep them involved.

Being available

The opportunities to meet may be rare, if not impossible, which makes it so important that you keep the dates when the team members have planned to meet as sacrosanct. Don't be tempted to say 'It's only a team meeting' in the way some do about the weekly team meeting for office-based staff.

It's easier to get people together who are office-based. You need to be adaptable, even when it's inconvenient, as to when and where you might meet. The inconvenience should be spread and sometimes you might be the most inconvenienced.

Disagreements and misunderstandings can be enflamed when people can't get together to resolve them face-to-face. So put in the extra effort to ensure early resolution and make yourself available to do so. It's easy to go to ground when you communicate online – but it's disastrous if this happens when emotions are heightened.

On a day-to-day basis

Acknowledge that you have received messages from others and follow up when your messages aren't answered. Don't leave people 'wondering'.

Although remote and virtual teams will share predetermined online platforms for communication we do still have our own preferences. Some people still like to get phone calls and appreciate the human touch.

With many in virtual and remote teams working away from a base or hub the pace of working life in other working environments can be forgotten. It's said, for example, that we get three times the amount of work done at home compared to what we would do in the office (if we are disciplined). So, even though you can send out lots of emails quickly, review reports, collaborate online with colleagues on a piece of project work and call a client, all in the space of an hour, this does not mean that others, who are office-based, can operate at this speed. Be reasonable in your demands of people who have to live with the disturbances, disruptions, overrunning meetings and mini-crises that are the norm of office life.

brilliant tip

Using Skype, FaceTime and other VoIP platforms that use cameras can lack authenticity. Making eye contact (great for rapport) is done by looking right at the camera. But that means it's hard to look at the person and you lose the subtleties of body language and facial gestures so important in effective communication. The limited amount of research that has looked into this suggests that, if possible, we meet at least once, those with whom we will have a virtual relationship, even if we never do so again. Do make the effort if it is practical.

I use Skype for coaching and find that turning the camera off from time to time means I concentrate on the words being spoken much more because I'm not wondering what to do with my eyes. I become less distracted.

These challenges are temporary technical shortcomings and will over time be resolved so that we get close to authentic contact using virtual tools. But for the moment, however, we are not quite there.

4. Effective relationships online

The absolute glue of relationship-building when operating in a virtual or remote team is *trust*. Trust can be built in the following ways when you aren't able to meet face-to-face to form traditional relationships and bonds.

- You meet your deadlines.
- You do what you say you're going to do.
- You follow up.
- You respond promptly to requests.

As we know, living in an online world gives an anonymity which is easy to abuse. Preserve the professional standards you would maintain in an office environment – don't let your standards slip because there is no face-to-face immediacy or because the boundaries are blurred between the personal and professional. People will respect you for it.

brilliant tip

Of course there is still a great deal of similarity between virtual and traditional working environments. Just as offering help and support in traditional environments is a great relationship builder, the same applies to the virtual world. Let people know you are there to help. Behaviour breeds behaviour. Do this and you will find that people are more willing to help you when you need it.

brilliant recap

- Be aware of the particular challenges that remote and virtual team-working presents - isolation, communication difficulties and maintaining relationships are three common ones.
- Isolation can be self-inflicted - be proactive about connecting with the outside world. Don't just connect 'virtually'.
- Keep your knowledge of online platforms - internal and external - that can aid your effectiveness up-to-date. Don't get left behind.
- Keep in touch with the team - sharing stories, feedback, setbacks and successes.
- Make the effort to meet for real if possible - it makes the virtual relationship so much stronger.
- Trust is the basis on which online relationships thrive - meet your commitments, be reliable.

Virtual networks

Networking has always been a wonderful 'opener' – for making contacts, building relationships, creating opportunities and 'getting your name out there'. In the past ten years additional networking tools have become available online that allow us to connect, potentially, with almost anyone in the world at the click of a button. Curiously this online facility has been named 'social networking'. Isn't all networking – face-to-face and online – 'social'? Many readers will have a presence on LinkedIn for professional purposes and some may use Twitter, also for professional purposes, as a means of building a professional reputation, being seen to be an expert and being in tune with trends in your industry. As we saw in the last section on collaboration, Yammer is one of the newer kids on the block, allowing for personal presence and online collaboration. Its great era may be just beginning or almost immediately something else may come along to take its place.

Many readers will use Facebook for personal connections (the professional/personal boundary can be blurred) although, at the time of writing, Facebook seems to be in steep decline among younger people as truly instant connection tools such as Snapchat become the norm. Of course, the danger in writing all of this right now is that in two or three years' time a new series of online communication tools will take over. Myspace or Bebo anyone? However, regardless of which online platforms you use to network, communicate and collaborate there are some rules that apply universally in a professional context.

In this section we will look at some key points about networking in general (which apply to both face-to-face and online networking) and then look at maximising your online presence using LinkedIn as the example, although the key points made about LinkedIn apply to many other online networking tools such as Yammer.

Online 'social networking'

Networking is a great way of connecting with people who share any or all of your professional needs, values, interests (professional or social) and motivations. Whether generating contacts and connections through face-to-face means or online there is a philosophy around networking that applies to both. Before looking at your online impact and effectiveness it's useful to remind ourselves about this guiding philosophy. Whatever it was in the past, twenty-first-century professional networking – online and face-to-face – shares five guiding principles.

1 **Be a 'builder'.** The best networkers 'build' relationships rather than 'use' people for their own ends, where the investment is for the long term, rather than an initial expectation of what you might get out of the new contact or connection.

2 **Active rather than passive.** You can of course be present on virtual/social networking sites such as LinkedIn and Facebook without being active but the real value comes from social proactivity. This means offering help, support, information and advice. Just as it does in the physical world.

3 **Behaviour breeds behaviour.** As has been said, networking is based on building relationships but you do get back what you give. Sometimes the payback comes in strange, interesting and unexpected ways and from surprising sources.

4 **Good maintenance.** Keep your professional image up to date – online this means your profile and all that comes with this (read further on in this section). Face-to-face it means keeping in touch, looking people up, sharing a coffee and offering help and support. Even just a simple 'Hi, how are things going?' opening up in the message box gets people talking about themselves – which most of us rather enjoy.

5 **Open-mindedness**. Don't limit your connections to the narrow confines of your industry. Weird and wonderful opportunities come from left-field connections. As the author of *The Surrealist Manifesto*, André Breton, once said, powerful ideas come from the previously unconnected things – the bigger the difference the bigger the spark.

brilliant tip

A truly altruistic activity in networking is that of bringing people together who might be able to help each other. It's a wonderful way to cement relationships with both parties and – though this should not be the reason for doing it – the stories are many about how the introducer benefits.

Your online impact

LinkedIn is, it is said, the world's largest recruitment agency. But it is so much more than that. It provides a great vehicle for professional impact and effectiveness across the whole of your career. To use it to best effect, you need to see yourself both as representative of your employer and as an entrepreneurial figure within an employed context. Beyond the recruitment context LinkedIn is good for:

● making and managing your reputation
● making connections
● keeping in touch with trends in your industry sector
● creating professional opportunities through your online network.

First you need to establish professionally what you want to use LinkedIn for and this applies to any kind of networking site. With nearly 300 million users LinkedIn provides a unique opportunity to connect, in theory at least, with almost anyone. The old idea that there are only six degrees of separation between you and every other person in the world sits neatly within the core idea behind LinkedIn and other social networking sites, such as Facebook. So, do you want to use a professional social networking site for the four reasons above or for one in particular?

Your reputation

Reputation management has become one of the bigger professional development needs over the past ten years and LinkedIn is a prime vehicle for doing this. LinkedIn is valuable as a means of presenting your best professional face to connections and potential contacts but it needs to be handled with care and attention. Below are some recommendations for the development of your LinkedIn page.

Use the same care and attention when creating your LinkedIn profile as you would with a personal website. After all the two are not so different. Do you want to come across as a specialist, an expert, as a person worth knowing as you are being well-connected yourself or use it for more low-key purposes – 'I exist!'? Are you looking for job opportunities or are you positioning yourself more as an ambassador for your current employer. The tone of your profile should reflect this.

● Be authentic – the real you. People talk of 'personal brands' but people will not take you seriously if you are not the person you say you are. You are marketing but you are marketing something animate rather than a box of breakfast cereal.

● What particular skills do you want to be associated with – good communicator, creative or a great details person? Use evidence to back up your claim.

● What's been your value? How did previous employers (at least the last two if you can) benefit from having you with them? Include your achievements.

- We've seen LinkedIn profiles with spelling and grammatical errors and the thinking that this generates – *'Can't be bothered to spell properly? Where else do you lack attention to detail?'*

- Use 'I' rather than 'he' or 'she'. Using the third person sounds arrogant. You are personally communicating to existing connections and potential contacts.

brilliant tip

Many people are in the habit of checking the LinkedIn profiles of those they are soon to be meeting in a business setting. What image do you want to present to contacts who use it in this way? If you're blatantly looking for job opportunities they may question your commitment to them.

Professional image

Colleagues, clients and recruiters habitually check the online profiles of those who are new to them. With the blurring of boundaries between the professional and personal do take time to think very carefully about who reads what and what impression they will gain about you as a result of reading what they do. If you are going to include photos of yourself on Facebook in situations that might not show you in the best light, then make these seen by friends only and have a closed Facebook profile, which again can only be seen by those you want to see it. The horror stories of people turned down for jobs or being asked to leave their employment because of social networking misjudgements are now ubiquitous.

Do not discuss your employer on social networking sites, unless it's for positive reasons, and indeed it is strongly recommended that you avoid doing this in chatrooms and other types of discussion groups. Yammer (at the time of writing used by 500,000 companies,) and its potential successors share some of the characteristics of Facebook but it is used for collaboration and information sharing across a specified network. It's easy to slip into 'play' mode on a professional platform so keep reminding yourself that this is you in 'professional' mode not 'play/home' mode.

brilliant tip

If you work outside Western working cultures people can hold different views from those you are used to about the way that working life permeates other aspects of our lives. Western cultures tend to separate business (where we might use LinkedIn to 'connect') from life beyond work (where we might use Facebook). These boundaries are not so prevalent in other cultures where getting to know the 'whole' you privately and professionally is the route to a successful business relationship. This author works extensively in the former Yugoslavia and is always amazed that LinkedIn appears to be little used and professional contacts tend to be included within Facebook. If you want to have successful business relationships within these types of cultures you may have to let people more deeply into your life than you would in your own culture. The boundaries between the professional and the personal are blurred.

Connections old and new are the glue of virtual social networking sites. Here are some dos and don'ts related to connecting with and working with your contacts and connections.

brilliant dos and don'ts

Do actively look out for peers – not just people you have met but also online acquaintances, people you know of who may know of you and potential contacts who have been recommended to you.

Do
- ✔ Send a message to new connections – those you invite and those who invite you. Offer help and support and explore areas of possible mutual interest.
- ✔ Give testimonials and you will see that this is reciprocated.
- ✔ Join specialist groups that cover subjects that you have an interest in. There are several excellent groups covering innovation for example and if you have management aspirations or you are a manager now then joining leadership and management discussion groups will be a valuable way of keeping up with management trends, research and to get some advice if needed. There are millions of people willing to share knowledge (and to hear your experiences as well).

Don't
- ✘ Just use LinkedIn for your own purposes but also indicate how you can help others.
- ✘ Limit yourself to the narrow confines of your own industry or sector within it. Opportunities often come from unlikely sources so look to widen your network beyond the confines of your own world.
- ✘ Just talk about yourself – explore the worlds of your connections.

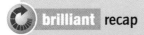 **recap**

- Many of the attributes we associate with the traditional networker apply to the 'online' social networker – effective communicator, proactive, open-minded, keeps in touch.

- Be a relationship builder not a people user.

- Manage your reputation online – be authentic, demonstrate your provable skills and value with examples.

- As a general rule keep the personal and professional separate.

- Share knowledge, industry and topic (e.g. leadership) trends, research and connections with others.

- Be open-minded about who you connect with and where opportunities come from.

Email and other written communication

Earlier (in Chapter 3) we looked at email from an efficiency point of view – using it for the wonderful communication tool it can be while making sure it doesn't become your primary time thief. In this chapter we look at email from an effectiveness and impact perspective – how to use email to get the message across in the way you want it to be read and understood. In this section we also look at advice on effective writing from a great writer – George Orwell.

To start, think for a moment about those annoyances you have with email you receive. Most of us don't have to think too hard. Once you understand what you find irritating, you take a big step forwards in getting your own approach right. Some have a tendency to hypocrisy. For example, some readers will have noticed how those who complain about how often they are Cc'd in emails are not aversed to Cc'ing everyone in the office themselves. There are several core recommendations when using email as a communication tool.

1. Ask, 'Why email?'

Email is one communication method among many but for some it has become the default method in circumstances in which picking up the phone, using VoIP tools such as Skype or a face-to-face conversation might be better. Emails are poor for decision-making and should never be used to avoid a difficult conversation. Saying 'I told you this' cannot be replaced by an email. It may not always be right for what is perceived as one of its strengths – instant response. You need to understand the person you are sending the message to because some won't be living in their in-box. Is this the sort of person who is slow to respond? Then you are better off just picking up the phone or moving from your desk.

So, a key question is, 'What is the best method for sending the message I want to send taking into account the preferences and style of the receiver?'

2. Ask, 'What is my purpose?'

Having resolved that email is the best medium to use the next question to ask is 'What do I want to happen as a result of sending this email?' and then make sure that your email is designed to achieve this 'want'. To that end there are further considerations.

- **Who receives it?** This will be based on the purpose of the message and whether or not you expect a response. The number of receivers should be kept to a minimum. The number of replies will grow exponentially the more people you send the email to.

- **Who is copied in?** Who needs to know this information but also, from whom do you not expect a reply? Cc'ing is prone to massive abuse. Who really needs to know this – even if it's just useful information? People will match your behaviour – you send emails to the world then it will send them back.

- **The structure and content.** There are mixed views on this. Is it like a letter and do the same rules apply? Some say yes. Others say that one of the reasons email is so attractive is that it can have informality and promptness when needed. Older readers will remember that before email we had paper memos flying round the office. The debates were no different then. The view of this author is that we take the same time, thought and effort over an email as we would over any other written communication.

brilliant tip

Can you remember the last time you received a letter that wasn't a bill or advertising? If you want to make an impression with someone why not send a letter instead of an email? Perhaps saying to a client, 'I wanted to take the chance to say what a pleasure it was to meet you last Wednesday. Our conversation really made me think about how we can work best with you ...' in a letter will make you stand out. It says that you really took the time to think about them rather than tapping a few words and clicking the 'send' button.

- **The subject line.** Create a new subject line for a new topic. A subject line retained from old emails, the sender having chosen to 'reply' to the old email rather than generate a new one for a new topic may mean your email not being read as soon as you would have liked or perhaps not even at all.
- **The style and tone.** Who is receiving this message? Senior managers? Customers? Don't assume that 'one size fits all'. This seems so obvious and yet the lack of professionalism in some emails is staggering – this is not a chat with friends.

How you express yourself in written form sends out a huge signal about professionalism that, in turn creates your 'reputation'. A good rule is to match the style of the emails you receive from the sender but the nature of the content will also determine the tone of the email – just as it does if you are speaking.

- **When you send it.** Not impressed by people who send emails at 9 o'clock at night or in the middle of the night? Don't catch the virus and start doing it yourself. Understand the working patterns of those you work most closely with. If you know that someone tends to check their emails first thing, after lunch and near to the end of the day, don't expect immediate replies from emails you send at 11 a.m.

3. Written clarity

The importance of good grammar and spelling was emphasised earlier (in Chapter 3). There really is no excuse for falling short and few things compromise professional image more quickly than lack of attention to detail. Imagine how a client perceives it.

Orwell on writing

What would George Orwell have made of email? We can only guess of course but certainly at least some of the rules he applied to his own writing, given below, also have relevance to the impact and effectiveness of emails and other written communication.

Never use a metaphor, simile, or other figure of speech which you are used to seeing in print

Certain phrases and figures of speech such as 'A chain is only as strong as its weakest link' and 'Achilles' heel' are so frequent that our overfamiliarity with them means they don't elicit any kind of emotional response from the reader. Think of the way in which spoken office jargon such as 'low-hanging fruit' and 'ducks in a row' were initially useful (about 20 years ago, and while I never liked them, some obviously did), then their continuing use made us think the speaker had no imagination and now we are so tuned out from them that their use has no effect at all.

Never use a long word where a short one will do

Big, long words may indicate education but they don't help ease of understanding which is the number one prerequisite of all written communication. Wanting to look intellectually superior is a micro-step away from being seen as arrogant.

If it is possible to cut a word out, always cut it out

Get the message you want to get across in the simplest, quickest way you can while, at the same time, looking professional. One-word emails are generally not professional unless that is the expectation of the reader.

 brilliant timesaver

I now invite my correspondents to respond with one word where appropriate, for example: 'Can you confirm you've read this with a "yes" even if you don't have the time to respond fully at the moment.' And the reply I often get is 'yes'! Perfect.

Never use the passive where you can use the active

Use the active. Avoid the passive unless there is no choice or ambiguity is necessary. This is the hardest of all but just as we said earlier (in Chapter 5) that passive words weaken the spoken message, they weaken written communication. 'Likely', 'possibly', 'might', 'perhaps', 'maybe' are examples to avoid.

Never use a foreign phrase, a scientific word, or a jargon word if you can think of an everyday English equivalent

The word to pull out from this, Orwell's final point, is 'jargon'. Jargon can alienate. It says 'inner clique', i.e. those familiar with the jargon, and thus excludes those not privy to the regular use of this private language and those who don't understand it anyway. Naturally, if you work in an environment that needs to use technical or scientific language then do so but be certain that those you are communicating with will understand it. Don't assume. Use of foreign phrases indicates pretentiousness which this author confesses he is sometimes guilty of.

 brilliant recap

- Email is one form of communication among many - use it for the right reasons and not just because it is easy.
- The purpose - clearly defined - will determine who sees it and why.
- Ask 'How is this email likely to be read? Is that what I want?'
- Professional standards with email (e.g. spelling and grammar) should be no different to more traditional forms of written communication.
- Follow George Orwell's rules for good writing - avoid jargon, clichés, hackneyed phrases, passive words and phrases, and intellectual arrogance. Keep it simple - can you say more with less?

What did you think of this book?

We're really keen to hear from you about this book, so that we can make our publishing even better.

Please log on to the following website and leave us your feedback.

It will only take a few minutes and your thoughts are invaluable to us.

www.pearsoned.co.uk/bookfeedback

And finally... the future

Gary Hamel is a highly-regarded strategy consultant with acute insight into how the organisations of the future will need to be to survive. As we draw to the end of this book it's time to look into this future, drawing on Hamel's work, so that you have an understanding of how this will affect you and what you need to think, do and know to be of value to future employers. In 2012 Gary Hamel wrote *What Matters Now* in response, in part, to the global crash of 2007/2008. Over the next ten years he says the following will come to the fore.

- **Values.** Organisations will need to be more 'values-driven' perhaps even creating what Hamel refers to as 'a moral renaissance in business'. Is he right? Shareholders have never been more active in controlling excess, regulation has tightened (though not enough for some) and social considerations are becoming a bigger part of corporate language. The rightness of your values will determine whether you are a part of this values-driven future or part of the legacy of the past.

- **Innovation.** Hamel says that 'without relentless innovation, success is fleeting'. You personally will need to think in new and different ways – always asking 'How can I/we do this better, cheaper, faster or fundamentally differently?' A new question we will all be asking too is 'How can we do this more ethically?'

- **Adaptability.** Hamel: 'Incumbents typically lose out

to upstarts who are unencumbered by the past.' Just as organisations will need to adapt quickly you will need to do so too. Be prepared to change and change quickly. You can still be 'you' – and so you should be. But that 'you' will to be alert to what's happening. You offer great value if you keep one step ahead. One example is to always take responsibility for your own learning and growth. There's nothing like new knowledge and updated skills to keep you valuable to employers and, for your own personal benefit, continually stimulated, rather than threatened by the world around you.

- **Passion.** 'Innovation and the will to change are the products of passion' says Hamel. It's why wherever you work you must bring your 'whole' self to that work. You will find it hard to survive if you don't. If you can, and why shouldn't you, work where there is the deepest connection between the real 'you' and what the organisation you work for stands for and does. Passion is a natural outcome of this connection and we cannot help but be effective when we get the chance to show real natural passion for what we do.

It is often said that we should 'seize the moment'. In the excellent 2014 film *Boyhood* the very last line spoken by one of the film's characters challenges this: 'I sometimes think we should let the moment seize us.' Of course, in the answer to the question as to which statement is right, well, they both are. To be effective you will always be 'seizing the moment', using your initiative, maximising the value you bring to your job and the organisation that employs you. But things are changing very quickly, as Hamel says. We are at one of these defining moments now – post-crash, with globalisation creating an economic sea-change and with huge environmental challenges ahead – it's so much bigger than you and me. How you respond to the moment in which we now live and the huge changes that are accompanying it will determine your effectiveness and impact in the future that is now evolving. Some people are rather terrified of it. It's actually rather exciting.

Bibliography

Introduction

Gallwey, T. (1974). *The inner game of tennis: The classic guide to the mental side of peak performance*. New York: Random House.

To do Peter Seligman and Christopher Peterson's VIA 'Character Strengths' Questionnaire go to: **http://www.viacharacter. org**

Chapter 1 – Learning and unlearning

Brown, M. (1993). *The dinosaur strain: The survivor's guide to personal and business success*. Polegate: ICE Books.

Colvin, G. (2008). *Talent is overrated: What really separates world-class performers from everyone else*. London: Nicholas Brealey.

Dweck, C. (2006). *Mindset: The new psychology of success*. New York: Ballantine Books.

Ericsson, A., Krampe, R. and Tesch-Rómer, C. (1993). The role of deliberate practice in the acquisition of expert performance. *Psychological Review*. 100, No. 3, 363–406.

Fenton, R. and Waltz, A. (2010). *Go for no!: YES is the destination, NO is how you get there*. Orlando, FL: Courage Crafters.

Gallwey, T. (1974). Ibid.

Gallwey, T. (2000). *The inner game of work: Overcoming mental obstacles for maximum performance*. New York: Random House.

Gladwell, M. (2008). *Outliers: The story of success*. London: Penguin.

Hamel, G. (2012). *What matters now: How to win in a world of relentless change, ferocious competition and unstoppable innovation*. San Francisco, CA: Jossey Bass.

Heider, F. (1958). *The psychology of interpersonal relations*. New York: John Wiley & Sons.

Jordan, M. (2006). *Driven from within*. New York: Simon & Schuster.

Miller, D. (2008). *Brilliant idea: What to know, do and say to make a success of your ideas at work*. Harlow: Pearson Education.

Miller, D. (2012). *The luck habit: What the luckiest people think, know and do and how it can change your life*. Harlow: Pearson Education.

Pearce, W. A. (1994). *Interpersonal communication: Making social worlds*. Harlow: Longman.

Syed, M. (2010). *Bounce: How champions are made*. London: Fourth Estate.

Wilber, K. (2001). *A brief history of everything*. Dublin: Gateway.

http://www.theschooloflife.com – I took the phrase 'you are what you are, not what you intend to be' from this enjoyable blog.

Chapter 2 – Engagement and effectiveness

Bandura, A. (1997). *Self-efficacy: The exercise of control*. Duffield: Worth Publishers.

Fenton, R. and Waltz, A. (2011). Ibid.

Frankl, V. (2004). *The doctor and the soul: From psychotherapy to logotherapy*. London: Souvenir Press.

Frankl, V. (2004) *Man's search for meaning*. London: Ebury Publishing. Originally published in German in 1946.

Maslach, C. and Leiter, M. P. (1997). *The truth about burnout: How organizations cause personal stress and what to do about it.* San Francisco, CA: Jossey-Bass.

Pink, D. (2008). *A whole new mind: Why right-brainers will rule the future*. London: Marshall Cavendish.

Rothbard. N. P. (2001). Enriching or depleting? The dynamics of engagement in work and family roles. *Administrative Science Quarterly*.

Ryan, R. and Deci, E. L. (2000). Self-determination theory and the facilitation of intrinsic motivation, social development, and well-being. *American Psychologist*, Vol. 55, No. 1, 68–78.

Seligman, M. (2003). *Authentic happiness: Using the new positive psychology to realise your potential for lasting fulfilment*. London: Nicholas Brealey.

To do Peter Seligman and Christopher Peterson's VIA 'Character Strengths' Questionnaire go to: **http://www.viacharacter.org**

Chapter 3 – Managing yourself

Kahneman, D. (2012). *Thinking, fast and slow*. London: Penguin.

Miller, D. (2006). *Make your own good fortune: How to seize life's opportunities*. London: BBC Active.

Miller, D. (2007). *Don't worry: How to beat the seven anxieties of life*. Harlow: Pearson Education.

Pink, D. (2008). Ibid.

Schwartz, T., with Gomes, J. and McCarthy C. (2010). *Be excellent at anything: Four changes to get more out of work and life*. London: Simon & Schuster.

Seligman, M. (2003). Ibid.

Tracy, B. (2004). *Eat that frog: Get more of the important things done today.* London: Hodder Mobius.

Olé Eichorn's amusing and often insightful blog is aimed more at those working in ICT industries but what he says has universal applications. His blog can be found here: **http://www.w-uh.com/posts/030308-tyranny_of_email. html**

The 'YouTube' link for Marion Bartoli's brutal practice session is here: **http://www.youtube.com/watch?v=q4_EuSK4F18**

Chapter 4 – Goal achievement

Britton, B. K. and Tesser, A. (1991). Effects of time-management practices on college grades. *Journal of Educational Psychology,* 83, 405–410.

Brown, M. (1993). Ibid.

Draaisma, D. (2004). *Why life speeds up as you get older: How memory shapes our past.* Cambridge: Cambridge University Press.

Miller, D. (2012). Ibid.

Surowiecki, J. (2004). *The wisdom of crowds: Why the many are smarter than the few.* London: Abacus.

The link for the YouTube video featuring basketball players can be found at: **http://www.youtube.com/watch?v= Ahg6qcgoay4**

Part 2 – Introduction

Asch, S. E. (1946). Forming impressions of personality. *The Journal of Abnormal and Social Psychology,* Vol. 41, No. 3, 258–290.

Gladwell, M. (2005). *Blink: The power of thinking without thinking.* London: Penguin.

Wilson, T. (2002). *Strangers to ourselves: Discovering the adaptive unconscious.* Cambridge, MA: Harvard University Press.

Chapter 5 – Communication essentials

Black, M. J. and Yacoob, Y. (1997). Recognizing facial expressions in image sequences using local parameterized models of image motion. *International Journal of Computer Vision,* Vol. 25, No. 1, 23–48.

Borg, J. (2008). *Body language: Seven easy lessons to master the silent language.* Harlow: Pearson Education.

Borg, J. (2007). *Persuasion: The art of influencing people.* Harlow: Pearson Education.

Brown, M. (1993). Ibid.

Carney, D., Cuddy, A. and Yap, A. (2010). Power posing: Brief nonverbal displays affect neuroendocrine levels and risk tolerance. *Psychological Science,* XX(X) 1–6.

Coupland, D. (1996). *Microserfs.* New York: Harper Perennial.

Ekman, P. and Friesen, W. V. (1971). Constants across cultures in the face and emotion. *Journal of Personality and Social Psychology,* Vol. 17, No. 2, 124–129.

Grinder, J. and Bandler, R. (1975). *The structure of magic Vol. II: A book about communication and change.* Palo Alto, CA: Science and Behavior Books.

Kelly, G. A. (1963). *A theory of personality: Psychology of personal constructs.* New York: W.W. Norton.

Litvinoff, S. (2007). *The confidence plan.* London: BBC Active.

Miller, D. (2005). *Positive thinking, positive action: Essential steps to achieve your potential.* London: BBC Active.

Pearce, W. B. and Pearce, K. A. (2000). Combining passions and abilities: toward dialogic virtuosity. *Southern Communication Journal.* Vol. 65, 161–175.

Pease, A. and Pease B. (2004). *The definitive book of body language: How to read others attitudes by their gestures.* London: Orion Books.

Chapter 6 – Assertiveness and influencing

Back, K. and Back, K. (1999). *Assertiveness at work: A practical guide to handling awkward situations.* Maidenhead: McGraw-Hill.

Handy, C. (1999). *Understanding organizations: How understanding the ways organizations actually work can be used to manage them better.* London: Penguin.

Litvinoff, S. (2007). Ibid.

Pearce, W. B. and Pearce, K. A. (2000). Combining passions and abilities: toward dialogic virtuosity. *Southern Communication Journal,* 65, 161–175.

Pearce, W. A., Ibid.

Smith, M. J. (1975). *When I say no I feel guilty: How to cope, using the skills of systematic assertive therapy.* New York: Bantam.

Sutton, S. (2006). *Say it with confidence: The 7-step plan.* London: BBC Active.

Kenneth Thomas and Ralph Kilmann's website can be found at: **www.kilmanndiagnostics.com**

Chapter 7 – Working in a team

Belbin, M. (2010). *Management teams: Why they succeed or fail.* Oxford: Butterworth-Heinemann.

Claxton, G. Ibid.

Chopra, D. (2007). *The seven spiritual laws of success: A pocketbook guide to fulfilling your dreams.* San Rafael, CA: Amber-Allen Publishing.

Honey, P. (2001). *Teams and teamwork.* Maidenhead: Peter Honey Publications.

Miller, D. (2011). *Brilliant teams: What to know, do and say to make a brilliant team.* Harlow: Pearson Education.

Von Oech, R. (1998). *A whack on the side of the head: How you can be more creative.* New York: Warner Books.

Tom Peters' website is a goldmine of wonderfully useful material. Access it at: **www.tompeters.com**

Visit The Dolphin Organisation's website at: **www.dolphinindex. org** for more on innovation and the culture that supports it.

Chapter 8 – Working in a virtual world

Miller, D. (2011). Ibid.

And finally ... the future

Hamel, G. (2012). Ibid.

Index